LETTERS TO MY CHILDREN

by

Joseph A. Patenaude

iUniverse books may be ordered through booksellers or by contacting:

iUniverse
1663 Liberty Drive
Bloomington, IN 47403
www.iuniverse.com
1-800-Authors (1-800-288-4677)

ISBN: 978-0-595-52805-9 (pbk)
ISBN: 978-0-595-62859-9 (ebk)

Printed in the United States of America

to

Elaine,

Mildred and Arthur

CONTENTS

About These Letters   ix

To My Ten Children And Sixteen Grandchildern   1

The Disappearance Of The Middle Class In America   11

Pro Life Or Pro Choice   13

Capitalism Or Communism   29

American Hero Or Republican Myth   55

Healthcare   67

Social Security Or Private Accounts   89

Our Standard Of Living, Increasing Or Decreasing   107

Term Limits Or Corruption   121

Energy - Oil, Nuclear Or Sustainable   131

Republican Or Union Man   143

Are We Really All Americans?   153

Pessimist Or Realist   165

Our Children's Dilemma   185

FOREWORD

ABOUT THESE LETTERS

Many years have gone by since all of you were young and the world was full of promises. America, the best country in the world, where working persons, using their abilities, a lot of effort and hard work, could participate in a flourishing economy, creating the lifestyle desired by most people around the world. Now, fifty years later most of the opportunities for working people are fading into the sunset, many new jobs are being created, but many "older Americans", still working to make a living are being thrown out of living wage jobs. I am writing about the demise of our society in America, that effects every person like you and me, and will have a profound effect on our future generations.

I have watched almost every great American institution become demonized, commercialized, or vandalized. From the most revered religions, the healthcare system, our capitalist/industrialist/military system, political /legal complex, educational system and care for the elderly and the poor, America has been degraded by blatant disrespect and unethical behavior.

Everything I say will be challenged, they are my ideas of what 50 years of observations provide, empirical information that will be disputed as to the exact date, time, actions, people, and results. These observations are through my lenses and my brain filter, they will be biased, just as everyone else in the world is biased. They are not edited, for vulgarity or to "protect" the many people who will be offended at hearing my version of the truth. So do not take these statements as the final say, your word or opinion is as good as mine.

Many people will say these LETTERS are sacrilegious, others will say its blasphemy, communistic, socialistic, others just plain insane. I say they are letters, written to my children, who are now adults with adult children, and to all children, 50 years and younger, who have been betrayed by a world turned up side down, especially from events witnessed in the past few years. America, the greatest country in recorded history, on the brink of disaster.

Oil, one of the most useful commodities on the planet, has to be removed as our principal energy source, regardless of apparent cost. The real long-term cost is bankrupting America, while moving World Power to the East and Asia. Capitalism, the backbone of the free world, standing with One foot in Communism, the other in Democracy. Who or what will survive, a frightening thought, World Communism.

We are now seeing a $1,000,000,000.00 run for the White House where presidential candidates are spending 100 million dollars to be elected President of the USA, a job that pays about $500,000 a year. That in itself sounds insane. These letters make many derogatory statements, about all aspects of our present American way of life. Therefore, people will immediately start to look at my background for something wrong, to discredit or destroy me. Like the Bush administration does to their opponents, a routine we have seen many times.

Do not bother.

If anyone is going to look for skeletons in my closet, they will be surprised. There are so many, they have moved into the living room, and even that is overcrowded. My life has had many challenges. I married very early, had children, divorced after 20 years, remarried, had additional children. We have children of hers, mine and ours, 10 total(some still estranged from my 1st marriage, 30 years after my divorce), and 16 grandchildren. Now retired, I suffered a serious stroke, and I am in the process of recovering at 75 years old. During the days of marital upheaval prior to my divorce, I left a packed emotional mine field for my children to navigate. That is not a very good legacy, certainly not the Brady Bunch by any means.

Bad things, good things, all relative to what the circumstances were. As a working person with children, there were many tough times, for everyone. Therefore, anyone can freely assail me, but he or she cannot stop my disagreements with people who are tearing our country apart. As someone lucky to be alive for 75 years, no one can cause me any greater problems than I have already had. The next step is being on the wrong side of the grass, and I am ready for that.

I see an up side down world where almost every institution and leader is doing the exact opposite of what we would have expected 50 years ago, and the change is not making America a better place to live. When you include the new world economy, AMERICAN CHILDREN ARE IN PERIL. They have real and eminent threats that may destroy their way of life. Many changes have been brought about by technology, but America's problems are self-inflicted, by GREED, fed by FEAR, and a corrupt government. All of the things that America stood for, real freedom and equal opportunity, we have allowed OURSELVES to destroy.

There is a wave of a depraved process and immoral government, at all levels, it started in 1968, with the corrupt Republican Presidency of Richard Nixon and his V.P. Spiro Agnew. To start, Spiro Agnew resigned in 1973 over scandals of bribery, tax evasion and other crimes. Then Nixon, after many illegal activities of his own, including wire-tapping, break-ins, secret illegal bombings, was proven involved with this criminal activity. He sealed his downfall with Watergate and resigned, before he could be impeached. Republican President Nixon's election to office was the beginning of a 39 year period of Presidential Corruption, with a few short breaks from major scandals, with Presidents Ford, Carter and George H.W. Bush.

Every two term Republican president since 1968, has been accused of serious crimes against Democracy, our Freedom, their political rivals, or other countries. If we throw in Democrat Bill Clinton, that brings the sad statistics, of the last 39 years, 29 have been with Disgraced Presidents.

It is no wonder we have such serious moral and ethical problems in this country, we do not have real leaders, we have political whacks that appoint incompetent hacks, to run out government. The president's aids usually take the fall for presidential criminal acts, to protect the president. Republican Richard Nixon's crimes were so blatant, so serious, very much like George Bush's, that he resigned in disgrace. These corrupt presidents are NOT great examples for our children. Should we be telling our children to aspire to become president, when we have this criminal presidential record? Along with the immoral Presidencies, we have countless elected officials, government workers, corporate executives, union officials, sent to prison, convicted of corruption. A devastating blow to the ideals of America. A good career path, to the mafia!

Then you can throw in the religious scandals, pedophile priests, preachers soliciting gays for sex, preacher's mega million dollar empires collapse because of sexual promiscuity, covered by blatant lies, all while preaching in the name of GOD. What a degradation of RELIGION, our normal bastion of high esteem.

Today, to add to our religious problems, is the assault on our society by another religious group, the radical arm of Islam, part of the 1.2 billion member Muslim world. They are widespread around the world, and in America, they are protected by our "freedom from religious persecution" laws, so they can practice wherever they please. In America, we are supposed to be civilized people, Christian, Jew, Hindu, Muslim, or other, led by moral people, with respect for each other. We now have a religion that is openly preaching hate, while enjoying American freedom.

The Koran may be every bit as legitimate as any other religious book, but if they teach CHILDREN TO KILL, instead of kindness, teach hatred instead of tolerance, they should be banned from our society. Everyone in America is equal under the law. We have a choice, an American can be an INFIDEL! They cannot be killed or persecuted for not believing or honoring Mohammed, or any other religious symbol. Islamic leaders must change their radical teachings or be banned as a religion in America. This is the 21st century. Democracy does not mean we have to allow others to change our society to fit their religion, OR KILL US.

In 50 short years we have turned just about everything UP SIDE DOWN. Our American society has been altered so much that we often have more compassion for an animal than we do a person in trouble. Everything is mine, for the taking. And I want it NOW. NO, I cannot wait.

If we are a Christian country, how can we destroy a country of 30 million people, because they took 3000 lives in America? Is it Christian or Pagan or Pro Life, when innocent lives are destroyed to "get even"? Is it for our national security, when those 30 million people had nothing to do with 9/11? Will we continue this destruction in Afghanistan, even though the Russians were humiliated and retreated in defeat after a futile 10-year invasion of the same country? All this sounds like good strategic planning, for someone graduating from grade school.

In these letters, you will find the same subject brought up and discussed more than once. When you were kids, you will remember that phrase, " I have told you 10 times, to clean your room". So I am allowed this shortcoming. There are plenty of repeats. It is time to see ourselves in the mirror, as others see us and decide if we like the looks, of a different America. In my opinion, we need a dramatic facelift and a body overhaul.

The American Dream is being pushed out of reach for most people. Your children and many grandchildren to come will be denied the opportunity to achieve that goal. Any major change in direction has to come from our young people. Politicians, capitalists, the movie industry, educators and our churches, have betrayed American ideals, all with our assistance.

At 75 years old, you would imagine that I should have some answers to our present day problems. It seems I still have more questions than answers, that I hope will make our children THINK, we need leaders for freedom and prosperity. Lets start be returning RESPECT to our society. The lack of respect has influenced our current moral decline. Take some action everyday, sincerely saying please or thank you, I am sorry, I made a mistake or lending a hand to someone in need, that would be a great start. All journeys begin with the first step, let us start that journey for America's children, today.

AUGUST 14, 2007

TO MY TEN CHILDREN *AND* SIXTEEN GRANDCHILDERN

In a small town in New England and elsewhere.

Hi Everyone;
Our country, this great United States of America, is in peril. Everything that seemed like a normal day, has been turned up side down. Capitalists have illegally taken our jobs and have given them to Asian governments and Indian companies, to HELL with America. We squabble about illegal aliens taking our jobs, while we flock to the marts to buy everything imported. As always, cheap things may not turn out to be a "best buy", they have cost us big time.

Should we be totally consumed with 10 million workers from our southern border, and ignore the 1000 million workers in Communist China, India, Indonesia, or Malaysia. They are being worked at slave labor rates, causing the reduction in American workers standards. Are we trying to skin the wrong cat? Politicians, public officials, economists lie and fail to tell it like it is, the economy is in a recession, has been in a recession for months and may go into a depression. They continuously say the "fundamentals" are good, a financial translation, the rich are getting richer, the poor poorer.

Turning the label Pro Life, up side down. Politicians who call themselves Pro Life, show they are the exact opposite. Healthcare has been taken over by greedy corporations, doctors have renounced their Hippocratic oath, pharmaceutical companies write our prescription drug laws, all while our politicians do nothing but pile up lobbyist money and campaign for the next election.

The mindless War in Iraq, started by our devious government leaders, for GREED, REVENGE and OIL. They all should be arrested for high crimes against our people, sent to one of those secret prisons "that do not exist"(that is after being impeached, disbarred, whatever it takes). But we will not torture, just a little water boarding as "aggressive" payback.

Religions, once something we could count on as a solid foundation for personal behavior, have deteriorated to new lows. Deference, respect, regard, are no longer in anyone's list of options. Actions of Islamic radicals, pedophile priests, scandalous televangelists and preachers looking for gay sex, cast a dark shadow on all religions. Our educational complex is operating with systems, technology and information of the 20th century, in the 21st century.

Our country is plagued by FEAR. Our usual strong conviction that as Americans we are afraid of no one, has disappeared. Who keeps saying, "If we don't go there, they will come here"? We called them cowards, when I was young. Politicians create LABELS to hide behind, doing the exact opposite they promise to do. Like the Republican label, Compassionate Conservative, do you know anyone in our government that fills that description? "Be like Ronald Reagan", political rhetoric, about a well liked, ineffective president. He started many of the problems, for our middle class, we have today, deregulation of major industries, decreasing wages with union busting, tax breaks for the wealthy. A much less than great president, for any working person.

A steep moral decline in America; criminal presidents, criminal priests, criminal capitalists, criminal athletes, all who were once ROLE MODELS for our children. Parents are the only ones left, you had better do a good job. "Just say no," "abstinence," "the war on drugs," and other failed government programs, because they do not address the problems of the poor, the disadvantaged and our young people. Drugs to crime, unequal opportunity, hand in hand, they are destroying our future.

We are a country DIVIDED, not united, as we should be in this extraordinary period of a New World Economy. If we do not throw out the political dividers, like Republican, Democrat, Independent, correct the economic disparities, stop pitting one state vs. another state, North vs. South, and WORK TOGETHER as Americans, we will not compete in that new world economy.

Politicians always talked about tort reform and term limits, but they do not mention them anymore. They are considered insignificant, when compared to our other present day problems. Although all these things are major problems, America has a great entrepreneurial spirit, an ability to overcome adversity, and we can rekindle our love for our country and have compassion for all people. We need to refocus our effort and our spirit. All our children, in this US of A, deserve to live the American Dream, like I and many others have.

We are faced with a world that has drastically changed, FOREVER. It is time for all our young people to take the iPods out of their ears, put down their cell phones, stop playing video games and start THINKING. You are faced with a different world, where a young worker from China, India, or Indonesia, is looking for the same job that you want, only they work for such low wages, you cannot compete. Companies looking to cash in on the cheap labor and huge potential market, have left America. Only you can regain control of our government and regulate the out of control capitalists. Squandering your mental abilities on playing games will have to end, bring back American values and prominence with IMAGINATION AND DETERMINATION. Join in the new world of business, it is already going full steam, without millions of American workers.

THE NEW WORLD ECONOMY

A VIRTUAL EXPLOSION, at the start of the 21st century, has produced an effect greater than any atomic bomb or natural disaster we have ever witnessed. This explosion, is the convergence of several new technologies and 3 billion people joining our work force. The results have profoundly changed the world, creating an economic TSUNAMI, coming to America. It has already inundated our manufacturing jobs, destructively affecting the American way of life. Unfortunately, none of our "leaders" are telling us that this economic disaster is inevitable, it is well underway, manufacturing jobs as we know them, are gone. Our politicians, from all political parties, have proven that they are not leaders, if they were, they would recognize and act, to mitigate this impending calamity with retraining and jobs programs.

Improved technologies using computers, satellites, the World Wide Web, and the Internet, have flattened every fence that has existed since the beginning of time. Using fiber optics(high-speed cable for transmitting and receiving data), we have stitched together all the continents of the world, like patches of a quilt, to make a new world. A world without barriers between countries, except when one is imposed to suppress dissention.

The emergence of these 3 billion people, in China, India, and Indonesia, who have lived in abject poverty for centuries, have flooded our jobs market with low cost labor. One-half of the world population, workers, 100's of millions strong, tens of times the size of America's workforce, creating the new world of international manufacturing, where workers, often children, make a few dollars a day.

THE CAPITALISTS DREAMS HAVE COME TRUE

American manufacturing cannot compete with such low paid labor, our standard of living is too high, and to keep it high it is plain and simple, we cannot and should not fight capitalists who are outsourcing American jobs, we abandoned the practice of slave labor many years ago. (It is sad to say but many corporations and illegitimate entities still have slave labor in this country.)

New technologies, renewable energy, revolutionary manufacturing techniques, every aspect of our economy that makes a product, must change dramatically. Our wealth must stop going to the middle east for oil, and the far east for manufactured goods. People will have to be told the truth, so they can do things the "American Way", take control and prevent TOTAL SOCIAL DISARRAY, on our doorsteps today. Yet we do not hear anyone talking of this approaching disaster.

Our President, is unable or unwilling to recognize this impending calamity, or the other destructive events we are facing. Presidential candidates consume themselves with our illegal alien problem, how to seal our border, constructing a fence for miles on one border. What about the other thousands of miles of border, thousands of miles of seashore and far more important, our UNCONTROLLED, wide open ports? Billions of dollars for a fence that does not begin to address the real jobs or security problems in America. Instead of a fence to stop the flow of drugs, attack the real cause of our drug problem, OURSELVES. Drug education and treatment facilities would be much more effective for America, and our children's future, than a fence.

Companies that hire illegal aliens are not penalized even though we have a law that was passed 20 years ago to prohibit it. During Republican President Ronald Reagan's administration, when the same scenario for illegal aliens was encountered, "just" a few million less, they passed a law to prevent businesses from hiring illegals. We should be looking at the source of the problem, HIRING illegal aliens! With a 10-cent pen, we could save billions of dollars, employers simply have to write on their hiring documents, do not hire illegals - period! Well we know that will not work, Republicans have to support their base, corporate America. Private enterprise makes America go, we cannot do it without them, but it must be CONTROLLED and corporations and Republicans detest control, except when it benefits them. Why are we putting all the blame for our jobs problem on illegal aliens who have come to America? This Republican administration is committing a crime by not enforcing federal laws, then aiding and abetting corporations that hire these illegals. Where does the hypocrisy end?

And all of that is to prevent illegal aliens from taking what is left of American jobs. They work for one-half the wages our workers need to make, but they do the hard work. However, everyone knows that the real problem is not the illegals in America, it is the American companies who ignore the law, sometimes they even flaunt the laws. And way above all of that, they are sending our jobs where workers have no choice, and work as 21st century slaves. Anyone talking about the country receiving most of our jobs, sent there by our Republican/capitalist friends. How about COMMUNIST China! Is that part of this Presidents plan of spreading Democracy? Should we help and support COMMUNISM? We are sending America's manufacturing capabilities to enhance China's military might, already one of the largest in the world. Not a whisper of caution from President Bush.

MADE IN AMERICA LABELS, are they gone forever? Anyone remember Sam Walton's book, Made In America? Yep, the same Sam Walton whose family now runs the retail mart that he started, among the largest in the world. The new source of their products? MADE IN COMMUNIST CHINA, for the most part. Poor Sam, and he thought he left an American legacy.

Then we have every Republican and their presidential candidates talking about Ronald Reagan, as if he was another George Washington or Abe Lincoln. About whom are they talking? If it is the President Ronald Reagan I remember, they must have been living under a stone, they were still in diapers, or they are doing the usual, lie. Reagan 101 as some call it, must be how NOT to be a leader. He was not a great President! Ranked 22 second out of 42 by a survey of academic historians and political scientists. Not even semi-great.

OUR AMERICAN FINANCIAL PLIGHT

Anyone talking about your new landlord? You know, the people that hold your mortgage. It may have been bundled into one of those great Wall Street products and sold to the people with the new and improved oil wealth. Or maybe it was bought by one of those "American Financial Institutions" that are in such deep trouble they are being bailed out by Communist and Arab governments. Will Osama Bin Laden be coming around to collect the rent, his Saudi Arabian homeland may hold the note? Or it might be included in the trillions of dollars we owe Communist China. Mr. Wang or Mr. Yang may be calling in the morning to collect the rent.

AMERICA'S MILITARY

Let's take a minute to look at the greatest military in the world, the military of the United States of America. Has this administration so bungled everything, including the war in Iraq, that our military is at the breaking point? When was the last time we had fathers with two or three young children fighting in a war? World War II? Over 60 years ago? When were soldiers, some that are 50 years old, demanded to leave their families, for 15 months, then another 15, and another 15. How has the National Guard become the Foreign Legion? They were not trained for combat in foreign countries, they are the NATIONAL guard for OUR nation, not other countries. They say they should have expected to be called into the active service, that is nonsense.

Since when is receiving a "bonus" worth thousands of dollars to join, called volunteering? An ALL VOLUNTEER Army? In sports that would be called CRIMINAL. Add calling this an all volunteer military, when 180,000 brave people are in the service of our country, and 180,000 are private contractors, in the war zone, doing what used to be military jobs. Military support personnel, outsourced, the epitome of stupidity.

How has our country deteriorated to the point that we have to hire contractors to perform military jobs, working side by side with our servicemen and women? What phase of outsourcing was that? The tragedy is that the civilians are paid 4 times more than the military. Imagine the impact on the MORAL of our soldiers, knowing they are risking their lives while being shortchanged by our government. What about the cost of all those contractors' bills? Who is keeping tab? I hope it is not the same people that got us into this quagmire. If they are the same people, when will America be declared bankrupt? Or are we there already?

Here we are, in the middle of a minefield, in the middle of Bagdad, in the middle of Iraq, no idea how we got here or how to get out. We were brought here by our President whose chief foreign advisor was Prince Bandar of Saudi Arabia. What should be the most important thing to do in the middle east? Why protect "the oil supply" of course. SUV's don't run on raindrops you know. "Our economy and indeed that of the entire world would be threatened if the mid-east oil supply was cut off." Don't you remember the decider telling you that, over and over?

Another revolting reason to be in Iraq, commonly used by this President and all those supporting the war, "If we don't fight them in Iraq we will fight them in America."

So does that mean we keep sending our future, our brave young men and women, to be slaughtered in Iraq? It is like having a wild beast that will break out of its cage if you do not feed it humans, our soldiers and marines. If the beast does not get enough soldiers in Iraq, will it walk on water until it gets to America? Is that our reason to be in Iraq? What happened to the macho President who said, "bring them on"? Does that only apply to places where HE is 3000 miles away from them? Of course it does!

And today, ONLY a few soldiers a week, killed, and that is considered "ACCEPTABLE" by this administration, a truly disgusting stance. IT IS TIME TO STOP THE WAR! TODAY!

Now we have the Presidential candidates of both parties, taking their positions according to what is going to get the most votes from the primary elections. The problem is that none of them has any idea on how to get out of Iraq without slaughtering another 25% of the Iraqi population. No one knows, because George Bush, by his ruthless, reckless and ridiculous behavior, destroyed the Iraq infrastructure, the government, the Army, police forces, and anything else that could hold the country together. What a humiliating position George Bush has put the United States in, the greatest country in the world, unable to execute a war against a country one tenth it's size. The real problem is we elected a President not capable of running our country. PERIOD!

President George Bush, his political appointees, his Republican cabinet, Republican senators and congressmen, pentagon strategists and military generals, all supporters of a foreign policy built on lies and deceptions, have failed to do the jobs they were elected or selected to do, are unqualified and inept as seen by the results of their actions. Everyone of them should RESIGN, immediately.

Most Republicans, the military/industrial complex and the Christian Right support President Bush and his senseless idea that we are spreading our "democratic principles" in these eastern countries. If this is democracy at work, I will take any other form of government that does not create the horror that we, the United States of America, have created. Any Christian who can support this mass destruction of human life and property, had better look long and hard at the results. George Bush won the presidency with the help of the Christian Right. As a Christian, I would be very embarrassed to say I helped elect someone who has NO respect for human life.

Isn't it ironic, the Republicans calling themselves the Pro life party, but they support a war with indiscriminate killing of innocent civilians and the destruction of an entire country, torturing, violating civil liberties.

That should be an oxymoron, A PRO LIFE REPUBLICAN. Will our VA system be able to handle all the trauma cases from Iraq, or will they be "just" another casualty, like the current/previous disgraceful care of our wounded military by the VA and this Republican administration? And our military continues to support them? Or is it just the generals and Republicans who want the war to continue? We will have to sacrifice, as we have done many times, but it will be a new experience for our children, who have mostly "had it all". Real sacrifice, and we must be willing to go the extra mile to help America return to its status as a great Nation, with real leaders for PEACE AND PROSPERITY, not war.

They are squandering America's assets on the war in Iraq, hundreds of billions of dollars, for OIL? However, the Iraq war is small potatoes compared to the disaster ahead for America. Please forgive the irreverent phrase, I am not belittling the human cost of the war, borne only by our soldiers and their families. They will be paying double for our misguided mission. NO, it is not related to Al Gore's crusade about global warming. That may be real in the coming century, but this is about here and now.

It's happening today,

August 14, 2007

THE DISAPPEARANCE *OF THE* MIDDLE CLASS *IN* AMERICA

Our workers are being pushed to the bottom by capitalist GREED, aided by Republican politicians, with tax breaks for corporations that move to foreign countries. Wall Street blooms while American workers wither into submission and have to accept lower wages.

That's capitalism at it's WORST. We are going to tell all politicians, as you would a child, its time they start working together, to create a NEW AMERICA, one people, without labels. Not Republican or Democrat, conservative or liberal, pro-this or anti-that, red state or blue state. Put down our political, religious and cultural swords and be like REAL Americans, work together, or turn into the ashes of a once great country. America has sold its most valuable asset, the manufacturing capacity to outperform any nation in the world. For 20 years, capitalists have increased their efforts to sell our jobs to the lowest bidder, anywhere outside of the USA. They have succeeded. Take your choice, how to defining our present day corporations, by Greed, Greedy, or Greediest. Putting profits above America's future, they have left the workers on the street, a street of no return, on what was the most powerful nation in the world.

America? Who needs their workers, we can make huge profits in Asia. Politicians have joined in or looked the other way, while the American workers have lost their ability to earn a LIVING WAGE. They will be shoved down, much harder, as the tsunami nears. Our agencies concerned with worker interests, everyone responsible for helping to preserve the American Dream, are either asleep, blinded by GREED, or are engulfed in HATE and HOSTILITY, that has taken over our political system.

Religious leaders join in debates, to heat up the rhetoric of special interests, some legitimate, some very self-righteous. Corporations, American and foreign, have usurped the rights to dismantle and sell American technology, the sale is in progress, very little left, anyone interested? Our future as a viable working class in America has been completely changed. Most of those rules I kept telling you, about working hard, get an education, be a loyal employee and you will be successful, are now "an old wives tale", without any semblance to today's workers in the world of business.

Our manufacturing base has been sent to Asia or India by the same corporations WE made rich. They have built entire towns, in other countries, for people who have replaced our workers. Yet they do not offer any assistance to Americans. What will the future be if we have lost the backbone of America, a worker who can earn a living wage? Eighty percent(80%) of all business in America is SMALL business, but almost all business is fueled by manufacturing, supported by research and development. Your new job is clear, take back America, NOW. Our working people and indeed all of America is being pushed to the brink of disaster.

LETTER 2

PRO LIFE or *PRO CHOICE*

Hi Everybody;

Divisive, destructive, devastating, disingenuous, and many other words can describe the way religious and political leaders use this tragic problem of our society, ABORTION, to divide our country. Most people have problems when dealing with this issue, and the last thing we should be doing is using it as a political football. Republicans use these LABELS to convey the idea that being,

- Pro Life, means against Abortion and they should be, FOR LIFE.
- Pro choice, means for abortion and therefore, AGAINST LIFE.

Very deceiving, these labels apply to one instant in life or death, abortion. Saying a person is for life should apply to all of a persons life, whether it ends as a fetus or a 100 year old person, shouldn't it? Don't you think that people believe when you say Pro Life it means ALL LIFE? Not only an infant and a woman in distress. Republican strategists use deceptions, say something untrue to make others look evil, everyday. Look back to the Republican Convention. Republican delegates mocking a highly decorated Vietnam veteran, John Kerry, with band aids on their cheeks, ridiculing him for being wounded while he fought for our freedom. This is what Republicans have become with our present president, defeat your opponent at any cost, right or wrong, true or false, it makes no difference.

They are using the same tactics with abortion, paint the Democrats as bad, as bad as you can. Use anything, whatever, to bring them down. This is the way Republicans operate today, be aware. It is hard to understand how low the Republican politicians and the Religious Right will stoop, attach any LABEL, to defeat anyone who opposes them, while they accomplish their cowardly deeds, for political gain. You guys know the expression, "divide and conquer", it really works.

Separate the voters, yes, it's about votes, not morals, so they will fight each other about an issue that no one can solve without all of America's support. Democrats, who the Republicans have labeled Pro Choice, understand the enormity of this problem. They cannot destroy yet another life in the process, the mothers, without thinking of the consequences. We need to come together to solve the problem. Instead, everyone points fingers, blame each other, declare they are the moral ones, holiest of all. It is a well rehearsed phrase of the Religious Right, who spend millions of dollars to elect Republican politicians, preach from the pulpit how deplorable the Democrats are, but do little to help women in need. Our society, with the help of sincere leaders, can solve this problem. We first have to show how the labels, Pro Life and Pro Choice are devious, used for Republican political gain. Stop calling people things that are not true. Be real Christians, work together for everyone's benefit, then we would be able to make right this wrong. Abortion is without a doubt a tragedy for the unfortunate who are caught in this sorry tale of life and death. These women and their unborn need all the help they can get, they should not be persecuted by Republicans and the Christian Right.

Did you know they persecute pregnant women in another country, Communist China? Yes, the Peoples Republic Of China, they punish women for becoming pregnant with a second child. It is the exact opposite of America, they have forced abortions. China, a Communist country with a one child rule, is the darling of Republican/Corporate

America in spite of the fact that human rights do not exist there. Do members of the Christian Right, who contribute millions of dollars to Republican politicians, have any money invested in firms that do business with China? Is any of this money from investments in businesses operating in Communist China going into the Christian Right coffers? *It is impossible to say no*. Almost everything you buy today has a "Made in China" label. Every industry in America has some tie to commerce with China. *You cannot escape!*

Is it immoral to make money in a country where the government forces abortions, and there are no human rights? President Bush imposes sanctions, at his will, for similar acts in small countries, too small to stand up to America. The bully has met an even bigger bully, he dares not say a word. Is this the Moral Majority everyone wants to be?

American business has thrown caution to the wind to be manufacturing in China. So we have to be clear, is the profit they are making "dirty money", stained by the blood of forced abortions and human rights crimes? Do Christian morals allow you to keep money made with your business partner, the Chinese government, who commit these crimes? We have divested our assets in many countries that have human rights abuses, but not for Communist China. Are the profits in China just too great to let morals get in the way? A conscience is what we teach the poor, not applicable to the elite.

Does abortion tell the real story of Republican values? Do the Republican party and its Christian Right supporters mean what they say about being Pro Life? Have any of the Republican presidential candidates shown that they are for life? No, Republicans are Pro Choice, it's a charade. What the Republican party does is talk about one moment of life, the act of performing an abortion, as being the only time in life's creation that their label Pro Life applies. Has any Republican or any member of the Christian Right proposed a solution to abortion, besides abstinence, and we know that is like playing Russian Roulette, its just as deadly. They think they have in overturning Roe vs. Wade. What a joke for people who call themselves intelligent, to think a law will make abortion go away. The "solution" is not overturning Roe vs. Wade. That is a simplistic approach used by the Republicans to divide the country for political gain. When dealing with abortion we have a problem that is far more complex than the American people are willing to tackle and it will take all of our effort and resources to correct this wrong. This problem cannot be solved by overturning a single law.

A pregnant woman is not a criminal, in fact, she may be a victim of criminal behavior. She may also want to make her own decisions, that is a right Republicans say is the basis of their party, making your own decisions, for your money and how to live. But in this case, Republicans want to take away her rights that will determine her future. We do not live in a theocracy or a communistic society where others determine every facet of your life. Should we be using the Republican definitions that are completely contradictory? Is it a single time in the life or death of a human that we are considering, why isn't the Pro Life label applicable to any living human, at any age, like a true Christian should believe, not just the unborn?

If Pro Life should be applied to every human, is the Republican party going to step up and support all aspects of social justice? Certainly, the unborn are the most at risk, but a child is at risk from birth to several years old, many problems in the early stages of life may become expensive medical complications that require lifelong care. George Bush says it is too expensive to provide healthcare for all children. He, with his Republican cohorts, vetoed, repeat, vetoed child healthcare while asking for hundreds of billions for war. Wasn't this bill, to provide healthcare for millions of children Pro Life? If Bush VETOED a major Pro life bill, and he did, he is a PRETENDER. Or is it another case of read the label, where actions show who the real Pro Life politicians are, obviously not the Republicans.

Where is the Republican party when it comes to supporting other programs for children? Starting with:

- Sex education and assistance with birth control for young people,
- Pre natal care,
- Infant care,
- Pre school help,
- Nutrition, food stamps,

- Help for needy single mothers.

Republicans do not care about such trivial matters! People are supposed to take care of themselves, period, that is the motto of the Republican politicians.

If the Republicans and the Christian Right or Moral Majority, do not support

LIFE AFTER BIRTH,
WHY ARE THEY SO CONCERNED ABOUT
LIFE BEFORE BIRTH?

It is politics, at the gates of hell. A way to divide our country, for political gain, nothing else.

We see a minority, Republicans, who detest any social program(even child healthcare), see it as evil, and try to destroy it. They have to tell lies, deceive, tell half-truths or skirt the truth so they can control the majority. Most people recognize social programs as an important part of a civilized society but they are defeated by Republicans,

a Republican minority, controlling the Democrats, a majority. It's the Best Buy the Republicans ever made.

Republicans and the Christians of all persuasions should ,
BE REAL CHRISTIANS,
STOP DOUBLE DEALING,
TELL THE TRUTH.

Perhaps the Christian Right, instead of building mega churches and universities, educating young people with an overt agenda, so they can change laws to fit their religious philosophy, should return to the old fashioned way of helping people in need.

They spend millions to influence politics, promote discordant propaganda and engage in hate mongering.

IT'S TIME FOR THE CHRISTIAN RIGHT
TO BE DOING THE RIGHT CHRISTIAN THING.

Like building and staffing facilities where women seeking abortions can receive help, assisting the poor and solving America's host of social ills. Do you guys remember what we learned in Sunday

School? Since you and I learned how to act like Christians, did all the churches burn down? Maybe the Religious Right, have Sunday Schools where they teach the new "Republican Bible" Bush Edition, edited by Karl Rove and Dick Chaney.

"Take everything you can, give nothing back and convince your followers that it must TRUST YOU." Who would doubt a President Bush philosophy, he is a man of his word, isn't he?

What is the difference between the Christian Right and Islamic Fanatics? Nothing! Muslim fanatics hide behind religion to commit their dastardly beheadings and killings. "Blame Mohammad, he told me to do it, it is written in the Koran." The Christian Right stands behind the pulpit, preaches in the name of God, and will use the church to help destroy anyone who opposes their philosophy. They may not behead people but they support a President who has done everything against American and civilized society morals including:

- starting a war against a sovereign country, its dictator might cut off our oil supply,
- killing innocent civilians,
- torturing,
- removing civil rights,
- committing perjury to cover their crimes,
- destroying faith in our government and our church.

"Wait a minute, you cannot equate starting a war with abortions. The Islamic radicals flew airplanes into our buildings and killed over 3000 people. They attacked us, without provocation. We are Americans, we gave it right back to them. They got what they deserved." Say what? Did you go to church on Sunday? Did you sit beside the President, a presidential candidate, any member of the righteous Christian Right, or Moral Majority? Something must have changed, dramatically.

Are we or are we not, a Christian nation? It was in a Christian church, where I learned that we are supposed to turn the other cheek when someone does you wrong. Has every speck of decency, been driven from our society? Has Christianity fallen to using bigotry, intolerance, and prejudice to support political gains? Republicans claim they are Christians, on the high road. Christian must need a new definition in the dictionary when they use the label "compassionate conservative" for our present President . WOW! New heights for deceit.

A pregnant woman needs healthcare, child placement alternatives, someone she can count on to assist her and her unborn child. She may see that there are other alternatives to abortion. Once an alternative to abortion is chosen, we need to support the mother to be and the child. The Christian Right and the Evangelicals will fight for the Republicans, who are against providing this care, are those Christian actions? They say someone should provide this care. Who?

Until unwanted pregnancies are eliminated through education and prevention, we need to provide a workable solution, not a law to criminalize pregnant women. Abortion has been used as a wedge by the Republican party for decades. It has divided modern America like no other issue, that is until Iraq. Now the Republican horizon has shifted to a disaster they created, and refuse to stop. This unjust war, is killing and maiming 100's of thousands of people and displacing millions of Iraqi citizens. Are these the values of the Christian Right? Do they believe innocent people should be slaughtered because an irresponsible Republican President that controls our military, has made a horrific mistake?

IS IT A BIGGER CRIME,
A SIN AGAINST HUMANITY,
TO PERFORM AN ABORTION
OR TO PUT A GUN TO SOMEONE'S HEAD AND
BLOW HIS BRAINS TO SMITHEREENS?

Only YOU can answer that! THINK! If we devoted 1% of the money we are squandering in Iraq, on the abortion problem, we could have helped millions of distressed women and their unborn. Does America care? We must care if we want to be a civilized society.

Another question needs to be asked. Where are the compassionate conservatives and the Religious Right(and others of that ilk) when a women needs help during a pregnancy? Do they come forth, like all good Christians should, and say, "Give me your babies, you cannot discard them, we will take them and provide for them", even if they are:

- Crack babies, who will forever be brain damaged. They may never know a "normal" life.
- Children having children, kids without parental supervision. Now we have 2 children without guidance.
- Young girls who make a mistake, should they spend their lifetime paying for an act of passion, driven by what they think is "real love"?
- Babies of a mentally deficient parent. Will you put them in an institution if they are also shown to be mentally deficient? Can that still be called Pro Life?
- Physically deficient, a life long commitment of care just to do the things we call normal, feed, dress, bath. A huge commitment that many Americans gladly accept today for those less fortunate, an honest to God person who is FOR life.
- Babies that have health problems, known before birth. They will be born with serious deficiencies, the ultrasound shows it. This baby will require millions of dollars for care, lasting a lifetime, but Republicans vote against healthcare bills in congress. Isn't that a contradiction of principals? Or is it another selective moral conviction?
- Premature babies, requiring countless hours of care and total medical support, may last for your lifetime and beyond. Who will be there after you? Who will pay for their care? Is that a Republican concern, or will the millions of dollars for medical care bankrupt the parents, physically and emotionally?

"We are all Gods children and we will treat everyone with compassion", a familiar quote of many religious leaders. "We are religious people, we will spend our mega millions of dollars, taking care of the unborn and the unwanted infants." A quote you may hear, but never see any action as a result. Sermons from religious leaders, like the very political Christian Right, the Moral Majority, Evangelicals, Catholic or others, fiercely defending their positions to stop abortion, at any cost.

Is killing a fetus to prevent killing another person, the mother, OK? Does killing the mother, she will die if she proceeds with the pregnancy, make it morally correct to kill? They mislead voters, they fight to defeat any effort to help pregnant women and spend millions to change the abortion law. Throwing out Roe vs. Wade, will ensure a pregnant woman seeking an abortion, and her doctor, will become criminals and will be sent to jail. Many people think that is good! I believe we need a solution, one that brings our society together, not tears it apart.

If the woman obeys her Christian religious rules, she will have a baby. Will these same religious leaders make sure mother and baby have the care they will need? Politicians they support, most certainly do not and will not. Republicans, the loudest when talking about this calamity, use the issue for political games, a travesty on a travesty. But of course, they are absolutely opposed to any kind of social program for a pregnant woman, or anyone else who may need help. Welcome to the world of the righteous religious.

Let's try these suggestions:

"We will instruct our millions of faithful to send all their contributions, normally used for political campaigns, to help mothers with the birth and caring of these babies, nothing to fund Religious Right, Moral Majority, or any other political endeavors." Or, "On Sunday, every person attending church, will sign up and take in a baby that was going to be aborted. No questions asked. Millions of families, far more than those being aborted, a baby for every family that has the resources to raise a child." The Religious Right has many affluent families, there should be no financial issues whatsoever.

You want ME, to do WHAT? Do you have the guts, our righteous friends? Or are you a Christian, only on Sunday, or in name only? Where are the compassionate conservatives?

Not to be found. Where are the Religious zealots? Standing behind the conservatives.

How can teenagers and young people, who are constantly bombarded by every form of sexual deviance, that is portrayed as being a great experience, be expected to do the exact opposite, and be ABNORMAL? Sex is the major theme portrayed in movies, TV shows, music, on internet sites, every 15 minutes airing drug company ads showing how it is worth taking a pill, then you will be able to wait an hour if you are interrupted. And you expect them to wait how long? Sex is everywhere, even the majority of American people have an attitude about sex that is suggestive, it's free, get it now, with anyone, there are no consequences. Is that supposed to reduce promiscuity? Many parents do little to guide their children and teach them about the pearls and perils of sex, and how decisions they make will last a lifetime. Many do nothing at all. We are just plain stupid to preach abstinence as a way to correct our teen's moral quandary, they need a lot of help, and it has to come from the religious groups or our society when the parents are remiss. Sadly, that is where many of our youth go wrong, they have parents who are bad role models, or have no parents at all. A real dilemma for our American youth.

ARE PRO LIFERS FOR OR AGAINST THE CRONICALLY ILL?

We cannot leave this issue without discussing other times of life, the middle and the end. We have the poor, all ages, looking for a way out of poverty, just trying to survive. They have been shortchanged by the bureaucrats in Washington who do not care about people who live in poverty(not enough voters). Are the lives of the poor important? A true compassionate woman, Mother Theresa, spent her entire life working with the poor. Any Christian Right leaders eager to take her place? Leave your posh home and give your millions to the poor and helpless. I am sure the line for that task will be very short. If you are poor, your life expectancy is 10 or 12 years shorter than a person who has plenty of money. When Republicans vote against healthcare for all, are they deciding whose lives are worth living? Denying care is the same as killing, the results are the same, a dead person. Is that being Pro Life?

In the middle of life, we see many people with a chronic illness. They cannot work, their insurance is cancelled, they are physically unable to provide for themselves. Shouldn't the government and the religious leaders come to their aid? How can anyone support a political party that promises to prevent killing a fetus, but has no problem letting millions of people die because they cannot afford healthcare?

Is the Christian Right,
either NOT Right,

NOT Christian,
or BOTH?

SENIOR CITIZENS

And then we get to the last years of life, where everyone gets sooner than you can imagine. Democrats, in spite of the strong opposition from Republicans, passed a prescription medicine bill to aid senior citizens. A few Republicans actually voted for a civil, society friendly program, well almost. The pharmaceutical companies that wrote the bill, with Bush, Chaney, and others looking on, had to throw a "hole" in the coverage. This hole was to trap many seniors into paying more for their prescriptions if they needed many medications. A little extra for the drug companies, their profits are below 50%. I guess half a loaf is better than none, until someone who is truly a "compassionate person" comes along.

Is it OK to have a senior citizen, surviving on hundreds of dollars a month income, have to choose between buying LIFE SUSTAINING FOOD, or buying LIFE SUSTAINING MEDICINE?

Republicans think it is OK and consistently they vote NO on providing life saving drugs(passed anyway), they vote NO on providing increases to Medicare, they vote NO on providing insurance coverage for millions. And there we have the great idea that the Republicans and the Christian Right like to make about being Pro Life. Republicans are NOT Pro life! They are FALLACIOUS, actions are what count, not rhetoric.

The Republicans and the Christian Right hold up one instant in life, abortion, while hundreds of other times they turn their back on sustaining life for millions of people. They do not support any government sponsored programs that could make the difference of life or death for a sick person. "Let the private sector do it" is the Republican excuse, they can do the best job, if they can make a fat profit sure, otherwise a fat chance.

When people have worked for 30, 40, or 50 years, should they be entitled to live a few remaining years with dignity? Should they have the best medical care that they worked a lifetime to help establish?

- Who made America the best place in the world,

- Whose taxes went to support medical research,
- Hospitals,
- Universities.
- Whose taxes established Medicare,
- Social Security,
- All the things that make a great society, great?

And yes, who supports the greed grabbing government, whose members cannot work together for any common goal, except GREED itself. The stalwarts of America, the working class! When are the Capitalist Republicans going to recognize that a society is built on workers who accomplish things, not workers who are pushed into poverty.

How do the Republicans vote when it comes to supporting Social Security? They vote NO, and to anything else that will help the Seniors. In fact, all Republicans consider President Ronald Reagan their hero, every Republican candidate wants to be "just like Ronnie". When President Reagan tried to dismantle Social Security in the 1980's, he was rebuked by everyone including his fellow Republicans. George Bush, 25 years later, is acting like Ronald Reagan, he tried to kill Social Security, very Reaganesque. Is it Pro Life or is it Pro Choice, taking life sustaining money from seniors? It does not sound Pro Life to me, it's another Republican ruse.

CHINA AND ABORTION

And lets go back a minute to look at the country where the rich Republicans like sending all our jobs, Communist China. This country has a ONE child policy. This is not a kindly suggestion by the government that a family have one child, it is an order, a law. So what you say? Women are FORCED to have abortions if they have one child and they become pregnant. No questions asked. If for some very unusual circumstance, a woman is not detected as being pregnant, yes detected, street monitors watch everything, and I mean everything, she give's birth to a second child, one of two things will happen. The child will not survive at birth; he, she or they will be killed. A second alternative may be the family will be fined and loose 10% of its pay.

Another sickening aspect of Communist China's one child rule. Women bearing twins, or having multiple births, only one child is allowed to live. All others are KILLED. It would be quite a revelation if we could see how many multiple births there were in China during the last 30 years. And in China, if you know anything about their customs, you can be sure it will be a boy who survives, never a girl. That is now evident in their population, there are 20 to 30 million more young men than women. Where is the Christian Right outrage, condemning the Republicans for helping a foreign government, where they have a law that forces a mother to commit infanticide? Tell me please, any Republican, the Christian Right, the Moral Majority, Evangelicals, anyone, is that Pro Life?

This one child policy is of course for the general population in China. They have completely different rules for Communist Party members, something like we have here, the top 1% are in control of all life. Nothing like helping out our business partners, we are doing all we can to build up the Communist party. Again, where is the outcry for humanity that the Republican Party has for the unborn? Big business, corporate america(they don't deserve capital letters), Wall Street, the Republican Party, the Christian Right are synonymous in American politics. Helping murderers? Pro Life?

IS LYING TO START A WAR AND KILL THOUSANDS, PRO LIFE?

President George W. Bush has opened the proverbial Pandora's box by starting a war against a country with one of the oldest civilizations in the World. His knowledge about world affairs and history must fit in a thimble. Otherwise, we would not have mortgaged the United States of America, based on the ridiculous idea that HE can force the Iraqi people into a democracy. His idea that HE can change religious and cultural ways, learned from hundreds of years of tradition, with bombs, guns and torture, is beyond comprehension.

Our country and its actions in Iraq, all wrong and all covered up by one lie after another, demonstrates the same degree of comprehension and compassion that the President has for pro-life or pro-choice regarding abortion. None what so ever!

When a politician can stand up and iterate the following, they will be Pro Life.

1. I will not treat a pregnant woman as a criminal.
2. I will provide assistance for pregnant women, married, unmarried, poor, rich, black, brown, white or other.
3. I will provide health assistance to children, no conditions attached.
4. I will consider healthcare as a necessity.
5. I will care for the chronically ill and the elderly.

It sounds like a sermon you might hear at a religious gathering, you would think it should be familiar to all the Christian Right faithful. If you can HONESTLY say you agree with these suppositions, you can be truthful and say you are PRO LIFE. Otherwise you are, AN IMPOSTER, A CHARLATAN, A SWINDLER, A FAKE AND A FRAUD.

And that is my opinion of what vile deceptions are cast on the American political scene by the Republicans and their staunch religious fanatics of the Christian Right, Moral Majority, Catholic, Evangelical, whatever. Please, if you are a Republican, Democrat or Independent, when you are going to make an X, or a check in the box for any candidate, think about what the Republican term "Pro Life" really means. If you vote for a candidate because he or she "promises" to be Pro Life, will you also make an X, or check the box in your mind that says,

"I will do what I can to help any pregnant women, especially the teenagers, to get thru the heart wrenching, painful experience of an unwanted pregnancy. I will help in anyway I can, volunteer, counsel, contribute to a women's charity or just say: THE PEOPLE WHO SUPPORT ALL LIFE ARE "PRO CHOICE".

Just one last question on the subject. If life begins at conception, we are all nine(9) months old when we are born. That makes us older than our birth certificates indicate. Does that allow us to receive a host of age related items, like drivers licenses, voting, Social Security, etc, nine months before our birth certificate shows? Can your beginning of life and birth date be different? If it can, what do we do with early births, guess their age? It is a difficult time to be raising children in America, as you all know. My opinions may seem harsh but we have to Wake Up America, I hope you guys will hear the alarm.

To my children:

Please make sure our grandchildren know how to tell when seemingly good actions are indeed bad. From politicians to pedophiles, they tell you one thing and do another, sometimes with grave consequences. Watch the persons actions, their words may cause you to trust someone, that you should not.

Be sure your priest and your neighbor's pastor or rabbi understands what being Pro Life really means. It should be for all humans who need help, not limited to the sad event of abortion.

Remember - ACTIONS SPEAK LOUDER THAN WORDS.

Be kind, stay healthy and love our children.

Love,
Dad/Grandpa
XXXXXXXXX x2

LETTER 3

CAPITALISM OR COMMUNISM

Hi Everyone;

Well here I go again, trying to get people, people like us, to start thinking about what is happening to this great country of ours. Our society is going backwards, with one of the most troubling aspects, the declining state of the working person. We have gone from a country that made great strides in lifting the working person out of poverty, to a nation that has sent all LIVING WAGE manufacturing jobs out of the country. During the last 50 years of the 20th century, people had an opportunity to become educated, to learn a trade, receive on the job training, or simply be a dedicated long-term employee. They earned enough to be a middleclass citizen. They had hopes and expectations that hard work, using their abilities and being a committed employee would bring further rewards.

And it did! Many corporations and small businesses had loyalty to workers and provided an honest days pay for an honest days work. That scenario has been thrown away, the baby with the bath water, out the window.

If all living wage jobs have been expunged from America, with most going to a Communist country, what does that portend for the millions of people who once expected to be on the fast track to middle class and the American Dream? Dream on brother. It is now a mirage.

The capitalists have discarded workers, workers who have been abandoned by their government, they are without a single source of assistance, or a single ally, unless we, the American people, rally for positive change. Take back America, now, from the greedy, the uncaring, the enslavers, who are using the wealth they obtained from the sweat of American workers, to decimate our country and its future. By sending every living wage job into Communist China, India, or Indonesia, I shudder to think what children in the future are going to face. We have witnessed the dreadful conditions in Communist controlled countries, do we need to aid communism to be able to buy cheap goods?

Developed nations are not new to utilizing impoverished people as slave labor. It has been going on for centuries, but it has never affected workers of industrialized nations like it does today. India is not communist, but most of their billion people live in extreme poverty, where only $1.00 a day for their pay, would be outstanding. We should do all we can to help non communist countries, if we expect to promote Democracy.

Today, China and India are the new centers for manufacturing and computer software, established there by companies from every country around the world including our own American businesses. Pharmaceutical companies, computer companies, software development companies, telephone companies, call centers, anything you can name, any corporation that can make a bigger profit, not a profit, a BIGGER profit, has left our shores.

Loyalty? What loyalty?

That went out many years ago and its effects have been exacerbated since the Republicans took control of our country. Look around, see if any of our government officials are talking about the plight of the American worker. Was it or is it a subject of debate for any presidential candidates, Democrat, Republican, any other?

HAVE CAPITALISTS, WHO HAVE ONE FOOT IN COMMUNISM, AND THE OTHER FOOT IN DEMOCRACY, announced any retraining programs for their discarded American workers? I do not know of one. With millions of our workers being affected, our resources will be stretched to the limit trying to provide assistance. No one, the government, corporate owners, anyone who employees people, will support the idea that a working person deserves a living wage. Forget the minimum wage that is unreasonable, way below poverty, a slave labor wage. You have to earn twice the minimum wage to be out of the poverty level. The minimum wage is a political football designed to take the heat off the real problems.

The United States of America no longer has jobs for workers who could better themselves by working hard and being a loyal employee. Long term employees, with significant experience, are fired indiscriminately. They make too much money and their health care costs are too high, replaced by a person fresh out of high school, who has no applicable experience, will work without health care benefits and has no family to support. Is this the America that Republicans refer to when they say "let the market decide"? This jobs market is what you read about in the 1800's, when the capitalists decided "it was cheaper to hire people who were worked like slaves, than it was to own slaves." That is a note describing how the cotton barons used people 200 years ago, they had literally stopped buying slaves.

That bit of information is from the archives of The National Textile Museum, in Lowell, Massachusetts. It is suggestive of our present day corporations that are doing business in China and other undeveloped countries.

The vast majority of our workers will have to settle for lower wages and benefits. That in itself means a lower standard of living for most Americans. If the process is allowed to continue as it is presently going, with private enterprise choosing foreign countries to do ALL their manufacturing in place of America, we will soon have a two-class system in our country, the rich and the poor. American workers must realize what a dire situation they have been forced into, our government and "American" industry, choosing a communist country over free enterprise.

That is yet another up side down approach, completely opposite the Republican philosophy! Less government is their motto, but they went "all in", like they do in Texas poker, everything you have into the pot, to send our jobs to a communist business owner. By definition, a communist government owns everything. Just look at our neighbor to the South, Cuba. So what was our jobs are now directly benefiting a government, they are the business partner, is that a Republican "less government" approach?

We see many capitalist activities in eastern China, the industrial areas. There are Chinese people who are buying homes, automobiles, even becoming millionaires. Capitalism in China has magnified the gap between those who have everything and those who have nothing, its happening, even in a communist country. It is making class distinction more intense in China, far greater than in the past 50 years.

Again, how can the Republicans have such conflicting positions, they say one thing and then do another. They preach no government control and rush to do business where it is all government control. Am I the only one who sees this convolution of Republican rhetoric?

Do our workers in America, including the people who call themselves Independents or Reagan Democrats, realize what the Republicans and their heroes, what was once American private enterprise, have forged for all American workers? There are hard times ahead for everyone, we have to make better choices when we go to the voting booth, the last selections have produced a continuous disaster in almost every area of our country, except those producing oil.

As we see the 21st century unfold, skills necessary for the future work force are not even defined at this time, much less taught in our schools or universities. It is a colossal failure of our government, the private sector, education, and people called LEADERS on every level. We are in a global war for decent paying jobs, with Communist China leading the pack at the appropriation of American jobs. We are now helping a communist country gain political, military and economic power, something that should make this administration and our corporate thieves humiliated. However, it will not, they are shameless. Spread Bush Democracy! Help the communists? Say what?

It is a WAR on the American worker and he is without any allies. NONE. Not one. What has any government agency done? What has the private sector done? What have the educational leaders done? What have our Religious leaders done? Anyone else?

Nothing! Zed! Zero!

WE NEED NATIONAL UNIONS TO PROTECT WORKERS, THEIR RIGHTS, AND THEIR HEALTH.

We are competing with the biggest union in the world, Communist China. Shouldn't our workers be able to protect themselves, by the same means-with a union, from Communists who answer to no other government and utilize their citizens as slave labor, at will? Yes, that is exactly correct, National Unions, and to go along with these unions we need a New American Worker, who has the skills needed for the 21st century. Republican, Democrat, Independent, whatever, no party has tried to assuage the impact of billions of people in BONDAGE joining our workforce.

We need to abandon all the labels, come together as American workers, every one supporting each other. Workers have been given no alternative, corporate "America" has sold their soul and every American manufacturing job to Communist China, India and other Asian countries. An infinite supply of slave labor was too much for the GREED infested billionaires. They have replaced the American workforce, in total, with a workforce on the other side of the globe. It is a display of the complete disloyalty corporate America has shown for the people who made them rich and powerful.

Has a national effort to help our workers, by raising the education or skill level of American workers been started? If so, where is it? Should our country, that helped large corporations become the richest in the world, be given some payback? American workers think so.

At first, you might say all is fair in love and business. Again, the most demoralizing part of this tragedy is that Capitalists have dumped the American worker into a market where there are NO JOBS. They will now have great difficulty finding jobs with similar pay and benefit levels, for the type of skills they have.   These are the same workers, their sons or daughters, or their sons and daughters, that allowed the capitalists to accumulate their wealth. Not only did they help them accumulate the wealth, they fought so they could keep it. They went to war, World Wars I and II, Vietnam, Korea, and more than a half dozen skirmishes, everyone in America benefited from our heroes' sacrifices. Many lives were lost saving this country and the wealth of the same people who are now saying,

To HELL with America and its workers.

Our servicemen and women are fighting today, in Iraq, to preserve the American way. The war was started by lies, it will end at great cost to the average American, disastrous for our men and women in the service, all while the capitalists are benefiting from the dollars we spend for war. SACRIFICE? Not for any large companies in America.

WE SHOULD NOT BE FIGHTING ANOTHER DAY IN A FOREIGN COUNTRY while corporate America violates every soldier and their families, by shipping their jobs they expect to return to, out of our country. Where will their jobs be when they come home? China? India? Indonesia? SACRIFICE, what Sacrifice, that is only for the poor and our service men and women and their families. Of course, nothing counts, only MONEY, when it comes to GREED, and it will destroy them, if they continue with

- Their sweat shops in poor countries.
- Children and the poor working as sub humans.
- Swapping the welfare of an American family for the welfare of an Asian or Indian family.
- Giving our military and industrial expertise that belongs to the American people, to a Communist country.
- The only reason, profit, profit, more profit.

We have an economic and military giant, Communist/capitalist China, a ruthless communist government that does not recognize human rights, being aided by American and world capitalists, destroying every gain workers around the world have made for the last 50 years.

CAPITALISTS WILL RISK OUR ENTIRE NATION,
ITS SECURITY,
ITS ENVIRONMENT,
TO MAKE AN EXTRA DOLLAR TODAY,
IN A COMMUNIST COUNTRY,
DAMN THE FUTURE OR THE AMERICAN WAY.

This NEW global economy is controlled by international conglomerates, in collusion with many governments, including our own. Most of them are beyond reach of United States laws. They will be difficult to influence, and if we do not start enforcing our laws that control our imports, our economy will continue to deteriorate. Another fiasco of the capitalists, called the private sector and this administration, wide open borders without any hint of control or inspections. A Republican philosophy, let the private sector rule, providing yet another real life social and economic disaster for America. It is time for action, throw out the politicians who have allowed the devastation of America's workers and the unraveling of much of the fabric of our society. Major industries are creating facilities, worldwide, where they train every eligible person to compete with American workers, so they can make more profit.

CORPORATIONS and their CEO's are TRAITORS to American workers, without any doubt. Those are dangerous words, but the facts are overwhelming, we have been relegated to the trash bin of useless objects, by corporate America and our own political system.

Can we, the American worker, recover? Not standing alone, not a chance. Is it the end for the factory worker in America? Yes, as we know it.

We need new super factories in America, using robotics and imagination building select products, that will reduce the expensive imports and improve exports, and not war products like guns, fighter airplanes, and tanks, so our workers can build America for the 21st century and beyond. We can import products without stripping America of its great manufacturing legacy. Everyone, including the Federal Government, needs to participate, bring everyone together to transform America, to correct the injustice our workers are experiencing and prevent the complete decimation of the American

Dream that lies ahead. Republican President Ronald Reagan said we are going to be a service dominated economy. Did anyone bother to inform him that if we do not participate in any manufacturing process, we cannot reap the benefits that come with manufacturing,

- improved products,
- new products,
- exports,
- increasing our standard of living.

Manufacturing supports RESEARCH AND DEVELOPMENT that has helped make America great. What will make us great tomorrow?

You had better ask the Republicans, their ideas for corporate control, coupled with the plans espoused by Presidents Reagan and Bush, are a complete failure, like most of the other "let industry rule" conniving ideas. Our efforts should be without ambiguity, for all people, no hiding behind labels like Democrat, Republican, or other. We need a very different group of true representatives to our government, not the imposters and incompetents we presently have. Hey everyone, wake up!!! This nation needs new leadership where all the youngsters, that is anyone under 50, have to get involved, it is not optional. America really needs everyone. We have the schools, educators(if they get off their duff), infrastructure, training facilities, the World Wide Web, the Internet, and communications that have opened the door to everyone. Let's join together as Americans, rescue OLD GLORY before it is too late!

The world has been so transformed, that everyone is now close by, via the Web, virtually as close as your next door neighbor. Our ability to use Information and Imagination will be the deciding factor, will America's standard of living go UP or go DOWN? It has become obvious, to me and anyone who is not living in a cave, that there are no longer corporate leaders who understand the needs, or care about the ordinary worker in America. People who led large corporations, that provided decent wages, yes, a LIVING WAGE, health care, had defined pension plans, who cared as much for their workers as their stockholders, have left the planet. They have been replaced by tunnel vision executives who have one thing in mind, dollars,

$$$$, and with their name aside them, not yours. If we TAKE BACK AMERICA, we have a chance at needed change,

- American workers surviving without having 2 or 3 jobs,
- American families living on a one (1) breadwinner income,
- Treatment healthcare(not optional, it must be for everyone),
- Preventive healthcare,
- Children receive an education that will be independent of their parents income or status in society, and where
- Education will be free, from pre-K thru a 2-year college for all(trades training for those who prefer), 4 or 6-year college for those who excel.

All these things are necessary and can happen, when private enterprise RETURNS as a working persons friend, NOT HIS ENEMY.

George Bush says there are plenty of jobs. Yep, at minimum wage, a wage so low you need to work four full time jobs to survive. This President and his Republican cohorts, have defeated every Democratic effort to raise the minimum wage and they have fought the minimum wage policy since its inception. In any Republican controlled Congress, no increase in minimum wages, it is BAD for business. What about the workers, are they chopped liver? Now the new Democratically controlled congress has increased the minimum wage. It's a good gesture, but too little, too late.

As Americans, we have shown in the past that we can do anything that we put our minds to, so lets get to it, let's establish a new wage level, The Living Wage so a worker can support a family using the paycheck from one job, where he works a normal 40 hour week, a job that provides benefits. Let's put the United States of America out of the grasp of the special interest groups, greedy corporations, medical conglomerates and mega agribusiness. Let's fight for a wage sufficient for workers to support a family. Take back America for the workers, let's create that new workers union today, you need one good person from every trade or service group to start the process, it must be nation wide, and include all workers. By everyone coming together for a worthy cause, Your FUTURE and America's FUTURE, will be preserved. Power is the only thing that capitalists recognize.

Make unions inclusive, not exclusive. We are a country in peril, capitalists do not identify or care about the NEEDS of their workers. Extreme techniques need to be applied to the extreme problem of not being able to provide for your family, something Republicans consider unimportant.

THE MIDDLE CLASS MUST SURVIVE, THEY ARE WHAT AMERICA IS BUILT ON.

Billionaires, their corporate CEO's, our corrupt elected officials, will no longer have the ability to say "my way or the high way." We would have millions of workers, ready to support each other, an awesome thought. The internet and you can make it happen.

Nationwide, workers would get their bargaining power back, against every Republican backed corporation. An honest days pay for an honest days work, what an objective. It would be of National concern, everyone in the country would be affected, not just an individual company or group. Not possible you say. 20 years ago, yes. Today, absolutely, we can do it. The Internet can work magic when it is used properly. Communication via the internet, use AMERICAN computer workers to make it happen, everyone can participate, little organizational work to do, everyone can enroll themselves, no big or little bosses, NO corruption, on-line decisions, instant results.

21ˢᵗ CENTURY AMERICAN UNIONS.

There are many species of animals(including humans) on the planet that have survived for thousands of years by banding together, working to survive. I believe the middle class is at that point. Make the technology that is reducing our working class to second class, work for you or perish. Tomorrow's middleclass, yes, there will be one, if we work together to reverse our slide into oblivion. If we had strong unions, capitalists would not have been able to destroy America like they have done, in favor of slave labor. Start the movement today, everyone should recognize that we have been sold down the river by our Republican government and "American" enterprise, to a Communist enemy.

If we sit by and do not take bold action, we will have no one to blame but ourselves. Some work groups are still doing reasonable well, that have inclusive type unions. Most of these workers receive reasonable pay, good working conditions, benefits that include vacation, sick time and healthcare. Many still have defined pensions, an endangered species in the world of pensions. So unions are still a viable way to influence your pay check. But they cannot be done under the umbrella of our present unions. A new international workforce is seeking ALL American jobs, we will need the combined effort of American workers and a new style of Federal Government in America, looking out for our people, not the corporations(who have deserted us).

COMMUNISM.

Since most of our jobs are going to Communist China, we have to ask the question, do you guys really know what being Communist means? Having lived a few years in Communist China, we were privileged to know some Chinese people on a personal basis. Ordinary people like you and me, with stories of the brutality and oppression of Communism. Living in China was a very educational experience, it opened my eyes to what extremes a government will go to control their people.

China has 5000 years of recorded history, with many periods of great discoveries and great conflicts. The Great Wall of China, one of the few man made objects you can see from outer space, was built 1800 years ago, to protect parts of the country from barbarians. Feuding between provinces was common, a constant source of trouble for the rulers and their people. Territorial wars and foreign intervention, among many other things, allowed the Communists to take control of China and when they took control, the country was closed to foreigners for many years.

During this PERIOD OF DARKNESS, it would establish a brutal Communist government. They did not want to show the world how they ransacked every social and religious order, many established for thousands of years. They decided to remove any article or person that reminded the common people of freedom and provided hope, it was the sure way to make Communism take hold. They caused MAYHEM, with the destruction of every religious symbol, of every faith, Christian, Hindu, Buddhist, Muslim. Spiritual leaders were imprisoned and tortured, many for 25 years, so they would forget their commitment to anyone, except the state.

Violent Red Army gangs roamed the streets, literally smashing and destroying anything and anyone, including great historic artifacts. It didn't matter. Anything that could get in the way of total control of the people, was destroyed. Anarchy and annihilation,

- They killed innocent Chinese, if they had so much as TALKED to a capitalist.
- Ransacked universities and cultural properties, destroying anything that was a symbol of the west.
- Imprisoned and murdered dissidents at will.
- They created a mega Chinese Holocaust, not mentioned anywhere in the world press. 50 to 70 million people starved to death, as the communist government botched their cultural revolution.
- Churches, temples, all holy places of worship, ransacked.

A total spiritual atrophy, for all Chinese people. The complete submission of 1.3 billion people, at the end of a ruthless, blood filled Red Guard march, orchestrated by the Communist Chinese government, for the unchallenged control of China. This horror filled destruction lasted over 20 years. China after 1949, was like the script for a horror movie, depicting a 20-year march of ruthless oppression and death.

This period of pandemonium was not seen by most of the world and few details have been publicized. Living in China for almost three years, provided a slight glimpse of their struggles, with many stories told to me by Chinese people who lived through the chaos. We spoke with a Bishop, whose body was scared and ears mangled from being imprisoned and tortured for 25 years. We attended a Catholic church where stained glass windows were blown out, statues smashed, priests imprisoned. The debris has long since been removed, Chinese people still remember the chaos. We talked to university professors who were sent to the fields, for years, to be "retrained" so their minds would be freed of any capitalist or western thoughts. We listened to the tale of terror, told by an embittered man, whose grandfather had owned a factory in Shanghai. His grandfather was beaten to death for selling goods that his factory produced, to western capitalists.

Annihilated because he was associated with them. This is the country receiving our technology, our manufacturing expertise, our future. This is the Republican answer to letting the "market forces decide" what's best. Give private enterprise a chance? Not in your life time, they have blown it.

UNLESS THEY CHANGE THEIR ALLEGIANCE FROM COMMUNISM TO THE FREE WORLD, FORGET IT!

Is it beyond repair? I hope not.

President George Bush and his Republican know nothings should be banned, forever, from public office. There is a place for Government, but they have turned their heads while corporations have raped America. Give them all a one-way ticket to China,

including the corporate chiefs, who are consumed by greed. There, they can give all their ill-gotten gains to the Communist government. On second thought, the Communist government will take everything, when the time is right. Many must think that they are not communist, they would never do such a thing, would they? Answer the simple questions, have they changed their form of government, their total repression of human rights, allowed free elections or any elections, are their "representatives" elected or appointed? They are appointed, by the Communist Party! Do they still have a one child rule? If they are not communist, what are they? Certainly smarter than we are, we have given them all our assets and received nothing in return, only more money for the capitalists, and they are no longer American capitalists.

Visiting many cities and seeing the poverty was a very humbling experience.

- going to factories that produce products that did not work or no one wanted,
- using one of their hospitals,
- being treated by their doctors,
- visiting their schools,
- shopping for food in the local markets,
- walking in a crowd of ONE MILLION Chinese people, on a sunny afternoon, on Nan Jing Lu in downtown Shanghai,

and seeing how difficult life was for most of the Chinese people.

This of course does not include the "Communist party members". Their lives and their roles are similar to the industrial bosses in America, control the workers. All the current articles regarding China, still mention the local party secretaries, the supreme influence of Beijing and the central government. Do you have to belong to the Communist Party to be a businessman, own property, or to make a million dollars?

Communist Party members have always been the PRIVILEGED, better pay, better homes, better education. They must have expanded their scope to include capitalists to the ranks of the party.

Everyone has witnessed and can clearly see the results of a Communist government in real life, in real time.
- North Korea vs. South Korea.
- East Germany vs. West Germany.
- mainland China vs. Taiwan.
- Shanghai(before 2000) vs. Hong Kong.
- Our next door neighbor, Cuba.

All show the distinct differences between what can be accomplished in a free society and how a Communist society limits all aspects of growth. South Korea has a world class economy, North Korea is struggling to feed its people. East Germany was bogged down in the World War II era, it has been re-absorbed by West Germany, now we have one Germany again. It was a costly process for the West Germans, bringing their 3rd world Communist brothers into a modern free society. Mainland China had been in the throws of chaos for 50 years, while Taiwan has enjoyed prosperity. Many of the Taiwanese are people who fled the mainland, as the communists took over China. Hong Kong, under British control at that time, was also a favorite sanctuary for the Chinese fleeing the onslaught of communism. It became the business capital of Asia with their efforts.

Cuba has been Communist in spite of being ninety miles from our border. Their economy is mired in the mud that is produced by a Communist government, and it is making very little progress.

China's 1.3 billion people were in wretched poverty until America and other industrialized nations sent their manufacturing capability there. But consider this. Capitalists are using 200 to 300 million Chinese workers of the 1300 million people in China. If they already have most of what was our manufacturing capability, what will they have when they lift the other billion people out of poverty? A reversal of societal roles throughout the world? And don't forget, every other industrialized country is sending their manufacturing to China. As a result of the monstrous influx of manufacturing, Communist China is providing the recipe and ingredients for an international environmental DISASTER!

Everyone must realize we not only have 200 Million Chinese who have entered the new world jobs market fighting for American manufacturing workers jobs, we have 300 Million people in India, and another 300 Million in Indonesia, all who will work for a couple of dollars a day. We are talking about over a billion people, not counting our normal competition from the industrialized world.

A STEEP DECLINE IN THE QUALITY OF LIFE, IS LOOMING FOR ALL WORKERS OF AMERICA, AND THE INDUSTRALIZED WORLD.

While helping others is admirable, we can help others and still allow our workers to earn a living wage. Other industrialized nations do it, why can't America? FEAR and GREED are the main reasons.

Stark is the word that best describes what mainland China was in the 1980's. Around 1986, Stephen Spielberg was filming the movie, Empire of the Sun, in Shanghai. It was about the Japanese invasion of Shanghai, that took place before we entered World War II. When Spielberg came into Shanghai, he was astounded that they could film their movie on the streets and use the buildings of Shanghai, just as they were. They did not have to construct any fronts or facades to make Shanghai look old. It had remained circa 1940, 45 years later. They had to change a few signs on the buildings, but everything else looked like you were going back in time 45 years.

In fact you were, almost everything was from 1940. They had not constructed new buildings(sorry, 2 were new), never painted a building, repaired one, or maintained one in any way. If you walked into a building that had elevators, be prepared for a long walk up the stairs. Elevators in China, like everything else mechanical, were usually broken. No spare parts. No one would bother to repair things even if they did have spare parts. Maybe it was because no one cared enough to maintain anything. To me, it seemed like it was a land of "that is not my responsibility". That was Communist China's mode of operation in all the cities we visited during that time period.

Now we see the city of Shanghai being built by China as the REPLACEMENT OF HONG KONG, which was the business capital of the far east. They have transformed one of the largest cities in the world, a city of 12 million people, from an old and worn relic into a very modern thriving metropolis. An amazing transformation, of an entire city, in a very short time. Similar changes are happening throughout China. A great step forward for the Chinese people, we can only hope it will help lift them out of poverty.

For an economy to grow at the rate the Chinese are pegging, it takes a huge amount of money, energy and natural resources. We know the Chinese are polluting the air of their country by building "dirty coal" power plants to generate electricity, usually two power plants per week. How much pollution will it take to asphyxiate the Chinese people? When will their pollution completely smother our planet, or are we already surrounded by enough smog to kill off our future generations? Pollution in China was already at a disgusting level before this Communist/Capitalist revolution. Most rivers and canals looked like you could walk on the water, contamination was that bad. Some species of fish still survived in the water and Chinese men and women would catch and eat the fish, even though they may be only 2 or 3 inches long. Anything goes in the survival mode.

While the water has been putrid for many years, the air has always been filled with the smoke from burning coal. However, that was from coal used at people's homes, coal, the main fuel for cooking. They did not have electric or gas stoves for private use. Even if they could buy the stoves, they could not get the gas or electricity to use them, it was not available to the common person, only party members.

Like we have seen in every undeveloped country, "capitalists build an economy" on the backs of poor workers, with the predetermined results of the depletion of the countries natural resources and uncontrolled contamination of nature. All of this is so the rich can get richer and a byproduct, the poor receive a perceived benefit, maybe even an actual improvement in their lives, but at a monumental cost.

We see Chinese cities that are immersed in smog, air filled with the toxins from burning coal and auto exhaust, so bad that it has become a stigma for China. The polluted air is spreading to Korea, Japan, and many other Pacific countries. It is even showing up on the west coast of our country, thousands of miles away. If it continues, it will cover the entire planet, with a thick blanket of caustic airborne chemicals, a threat to everyone's health and the future of our planet. Is this capitalist assault on the environment going to continue unabated? When will the world put economic sanctions on those who are determined to destroy the planet, for profit?

But we have to remember, this assault on the environment is orchestrated by a Communist government, that does not account to anyone, in their country or in the world.

They have become the new bigger bully, that no one is willing to challenge. Please consider that all of this could not take place without the direct aid of the capitalists of the world, who are again throwing all caution to the wind, for profit.

How can the Chinese, a so called immerging country, build a coal fired plant to generate electricity every few days? It takes a huge capital investment. World capitalists, the stock markets of the world, with the "private investment" of the entire world, and the enormous supply of foreign currency earned on the backs of the 100's of millions of Chinese workers. These workers earn 5% of the compensation that any industrialized country provides its workforce, so the net benefit is huge gains in capital for the Chinese.

One simple example of how they are obtaining the money necessary for China's plunge into capitalism. Foreign investment that is being used by Communist China, for the company China Coal, is providing returns to investors of over 50%. Are investors going to pass that up? They should but they will not. Are we a free society that wants to remain free? Do we think that helping Communism is a trivial matter? Or does everyone now believe that Communist China is not really communist. That is a tragic mistake, and until the Chinese government gives up its overbearing control of its people and suppression of dissention, we had better take off our rose colored glasses. We should be looking at the deep red color of the Chinese flag, it's a symbol of bloodshed, in the name of iron fisted government control, that has been overbearing for 60 years.

What will the effect be on the world's natural resources, as China colonizes Africa and other undeveloped countries to satisfy their manufacturing materials needs? Are the new dictators of the world joining with China and Wall Street, to control world commodities? Or are all commodity prices out of control simply because of the new demands of the developing countries, a dubious thought.

Will we go about helping the Communists improve their undeveloped country in the same frenzied capitalist manner that it has done so far? We are experiencing a capitalist explosion not unlike what happened when America was completely controlled by the capitalists. We have toxic waste sites all over our country, many that have proven lethal to our communities, their children and they continue to cause cancer and other illnesses until this day, to the people living around them. They were left there by capitalists, who have a bottom line and nothing else. Capitalists, when exploiting the planet, exhibit no morals or concerns, no empathy for people, just give me the money.

Is Communist/Capitalist China going to be another disaster of let the market decide?

World capitalists are upholding the Republican/Capitalist philosophy, damn the people and the environment. They have flooded many markets with low cost goods, in the process, they have depressed all worker wages in America, and it must have a negative effect on industrialized countries around the globe. But there is a great difference, most countries do not permit their workers to be degraded by lowering their wages and benefits, it will not happen in a civilized country that knows the importance of a good, experienced workforce. They do not let imports get out of control, like our country does. With an incompetent Bush administration, appointing inept people to every position of importance, who are defining our countries policies and its future, it is no wonder we have such economic and foreign policy disasters on our hands.

We are in "uncharted territory". A communist country with shrewd leaders, using its citizens as slave labor to assist world capitalists, who supply the technology and techniques to mass produce products for world consumption. They may also fill the needs of some of the billions of people in that part of the world, especially a new market of 200 to 300 million people in China and an unknown number in India.100 million? 200 million? 300 million? Will the Chinese Communists have a resurgence of anti-capitalist sentiment? Now? After they have all of America's manufacturing expertise? When they have all the manufacturing capability of every industrialized country? When all of the WORLDS manufacturing facilities belong to the Chinese government, the only REAL business partner in Communist China?

Are the capitalists moving their businesses to China to enjoy the countryside, covered by smog, with rampant pollution of every kind? NO, the word is greed, nothing else. What year will it be, when communists take over the capitalist's assets, or will they destroy them first? How soon will they say, enough of the capitalist control of our people? Or will the Chinese people themselves rebel, causing another 50 years of bedlam. Not a capitalist concern, they are making money now, that is the only thing that counts.

Total is a word used over and over when describing what Communism does to its people. Everything is destroyed,
- your hope,
- your mind,
- your family,
- your possessions,
- TOTALLY consumed, depressed, demolished.

Many things may have changed, for some people, so these things may no longer apply to many Chinese workers. There are 100's of millions of people left out of this industrial revolution, where communist control is still absolute. Communists have a real mission accomplished, and like George Bush's mission accomplished, it was NOT the good guys who came out on top.

THE BIRTH OF COMMUNIST CHINA WAS A SAD DAY FOR HUMANITY

Saddam Hussein was a Boy Scout compared to the Communist rulers who committed atrocities in Communist China. Does this administration ever mention what the Chinese Government has done? Millions of innocent people have been destroyed in their quest for communist control of the country. Millions of people, today, are being suppressed by communism, in many countries. Communism in any form, is the ENEMY of democracy.

Communist China will not hesitate for a moment to destroy anyone or anything that is deemed a threat to their control. The Bush administration is too busy helping the corporations fill their pockets, while America is distracted by Iraq. That is the way it works in our country, very similar to a communist country, 1% of the people control 99% of the wealth. It doesn't matter how they got the wealth. By a revolution, or on the backs of workers and slaves, it's still ill gotten wealth. We may not be able to stop outsourcing, but what must be stopped is the transfer of all OUR technology to Communist China.

Capitalists will go anywhere that workers are paid less than what they receive in America, where they have no health care costs, they have no unions to stop work,

and they have an infinite supply of workers. That was the realization of a CAPITALIST'S DREAMS COME TRUE.

This arrangement is a boon for corporations worldwide. It shows how important being a good worker is to capitalists. NOT AT ALL.

We have a perfect example of how communism can overtake capitalism in our own back yard, Cuba. How could this happen, 90 miles away from the best place in the world, America? Capitalists once ruled in Cuba, not as a government, but controlling a corrupt government. They worked the people as slaves, they kept them in poverty for the greed grabbing capitalists, many American, harvesting and processing sugar cane. When the people had their fill of oppression, and with the support of world communists, including Communist Russia, the people of Cuba decided they had been slaves long enough, they took over the country. It remains communist 50 years later.

There is a town in Massachusetts, years ago called the Sugar Capital of America, because many of its super wealthy residents were sugar barons in Cuba. Their holdings were nationalized when Castro came to power, but they didn't care. They had made enough money for themselves and their next generations, so they could live comfortably for a long time. This repression of workers and the denial of human rights was what the people of Cuba hoped to overcome. But when all is said and done, Communism has again proven, as it has in many other countries, to be the worst of all options. It has put them right back to where they were, poor and oppressed.

The Peoples Republic of China has not changed its name or is ideology, it is communist, contrary to what many call a new capitalist country. If you do not believe it, look at the government with its unopposed oppressive ways and its tentacles of communism reaching into other countries. We have been fighting a COLD WAR with Communist Russia since the end of World War II, over 60 years. Yes, the cold war has been restarted, another Bush failure, never mentioned anywhere.

Russia tried to conquer the world by force,
- tanks rolling into sovereign countries,
- killing and torturing,
- replacing governments with their Communist tyranny,
- country after country going behind the Iron Curtain.

Thankfully, after many years of threatening the world with nuclear war, the USSR imploded, economic collapse. But they are coming back. They have shed all the countries that proved to be a burden when they were imprisoned behind the Iron Curtain. They are standing tall as Russia, with new oil wealth. And they have shown they are NOT a friend of America.

Who knows where Russia is going, maybe they will partner with Communist China again, this time it may have a better chance of success. Russia and China together(and they were in the 1950's), a people, power and land mass of enormous proportions. Their governments have only one purpose, total control of all societies. What cave did George Bush emerge from, when he declared, as he

49

looked Russian Premier Putin in the eye, "he is a good man". Poor George, seems he can't get anything right.

Russia could not prevail by force, but China may conquer the world by working its people as slaves, providing economic gain to maintain the largest army in the world.

They have total control over their 1.3 billion people, with 100's of millions that could be mobilized on command. Some gullible American politicians have said Communism did not work. They consider it a thing of the past. About one third of the world's population lives under Communist control, and they are fighting to establish footholds around the globe. Some of our politicians seem to be lacking world knowledge, maybe they should start over, in grade school. They have the audacity to say communism did not work! Sorry, but we have fallen into a spiders web, they will have capitalism wrapped into communism so tightly, like the spider does to its prey, so that they can always maintain

Comunist CONTROL. The world's corporate owners become deaf, dumb, and blind, to the absolute oppression used by Communist governments, while they are providing slave labor for the capitalist factories. Do they also forget, that Communism destroys Democracy. And ultimately all FREE PEOPLE.

WILL THE UNITED STATES OF AMERICA COLLAPSE BECAUSE OF THE RUTHLESS DESTRUCTION OF OUR SOCIETY BY REPUBLICANS, CORPORATIONS, AND PRESIDENT GEORGE BUSH?

We are faced with a TRILLION dollar war bill. Will it be trillions, with an s, when and if the Bush Administration is forced to tell the truth? Their illegal activities, when carrying out this Iraq fiasco, are unprecedented. We may be faced with years of national and international lawsuits because of the Bush administrations total disregard of any and all laws. It is the disregard of laws that distinguishes the Communist governments from industrialized nations. We have taken America down the path of dubious Democracy. George Bush has a proven record of disregarding our laws, is he imitating the Communist leaders?

Any American, Republican or other, who can stand up and say Bush is doing the right thing, when he allows the complete decimation of our working class, through "free trade", and our country to be degraded by his incompetent appointments, should be sent to live and work in the fields with a Chinese peasant. No, wait, you can stay in the USA, go to live with a migrant worker, in Immokalee, Florida, they do not have it much better than the Chinese peasants. The difference, migrant workers may escape from the horror of their existence, they can see the fruit of our Democratic society that they may one day enjoy, a Communist Chinese worker may never escape the tyranny of communism.

What a change of heart they would have, the Republican party would cease to exist, gone in a flash.

All of my rambling may sound socialistic, but it is not. In my mind, I have lived an extraordinary life that I hope to continue until tomorrow at least, with the aid of the capitalist system. A life I want you guys, my children and grandchildren, and every American born hereafter to be able to have and enjoy.

The good life,
the American Dream,
for all our future workers.

Sending our jobs to Communist China and India started the devastation of our workers. It will crush

THE AMERICAN DREAM.

- FREEDOM, to vote, worship, pick your job, all the things we take for granted, denied under Communism.
- HOPE, the foundation that Freedom is built on, confidence that we can improve for the next generation, denied under Communism.
- LIBERTY, until you live in a country where you cannot go across the city without permission, you will not appreciate the right to travel in your own country, denied under Communism.
- LIFE ITSELF, a loving family, good healthcare, great housing, what else could a person ask for, not common for the average Chinese person, a Communist denial.

We have to overcome fear, so freedom can be kept for generations to come. The problem is that the government our corporations are supporting in China is the most brutal form of Socialism. We enable the communist government of China to improve the lives of their workers, at the expense of American workers. Republicans are always talking about a Ronald Reagan government. Ronnie would "roll over in his grave" if he could see us helping the commies(and yes, I was there in China, shame on me, no excuses, even if it was my job). Do any Republicans ever stop to think about the restrictions the Reagan administration put on American companies that wanted to do business in China? If they want to look Reaganesque, 90% of the businesses and most of the manufacturing capabilities, would NOT have been allowed to be exported. Period. It would not happen.

At least President Reagan put AMERICA FIRST, unlike our present Republican President and his administration, who put CORPORATE welfare first, before anything or anyone in America.

To My Children;

We are at a very precarious point in our lifetime. Our security is now more at risk than ever before, the opposite of what the Republicans tell you, and that is supposed to be what they do best. Imagine, a Republican President, putting American CITIZENS and DEMOCRACY in extreme danger. Communism is making huge gains, much of it with American dollars. Communism and uncontrolled capitalism are the most ominous threat to the American Dream. Corporate America, supported by Republican politicians, are destroying the American Dream and what we tried to teach our children, work hard and you will be successful. That phrase is now assigned to the "in the old days" category, hard work for most of our workers is proving to be unimportant when your capitalist bosses have nothing but greed on their mind.

While I believe National Unions for workers are one solution to our workers dilemma, many of our unions need drastic reform. Teacher tenure, exclusive unions, government civil servants and the 20 year retirement standard, come to mind as things that need to be changed. So unions are a double edged sword, we need to insure that we control them, they do not control us, like Communism does to its people. We need to renew our efforts to be truthful, and to stop our present government and its criminal ways. It really is a matter of LIFE OR DEATH, for the American Dream and DEMOCRACY.

Be happy, stay healthy and be kind,

Love,
Dad/Grandpa,
XXXXXXXXXX X2

LETTER 4

AMERICAN HERO OR *REPUBLICAN MYTH*

HOW THE REPUBLICANS ARE TRYING TO APPEAR LIKE RONALD REAGAN, REAGANESQUE.

Hi Everyone;

President Ronald Reagan was one of the most admired presidents of modern history. His ability to charm, enrapture an audience, create a good feeling when there should not be one, was better than any president before him. It was probably the result of his acting career. I remember him as the announcer for General Electric Theater and the host of Death Valley Days, both on television.

Republicans want to emulate him because he convinced Democrats, especially those who work for a living, to commit ECONOMIC SUICIDE. They bought their own noose and hung themselves, by voting for the people and ideals of the Republican party. That's why all Republicans want to return to the days of Ronald Reagan; he convinced Democrats to support a philosophy that reduced workers wages(through union busting) and reduced government spending by making massive domestic budget cuts, aimed at the same Democrats that helped him into office. While expanding military and defense spending to keep his industrial friends happy, he fought against many other needs of the ordinary American worker. Take a look at where our workers are today with Ronnie's legacy, a very sad sight for America's future. Independents be careful, you helped elect him and George Bush, whose economic policies are the same as President Reagan, and policies will not change if you elect another Republican as President, it will be A Republican continuum of economic and social disasters for the WORKING person. Guaranteed. Voting for President is voting for your ideals. What do you want America to be? For everyone or for the rich? America needs a strong middle class earning a living wage, supported by a Democracy that includes all people. That is what most people want in America. We do not want a continuation of treacherous Republican philosophies.

- Damn the workers.
- Provide corporate welfare and give the rich tax breaks.
- Do not provide help for the poor.
- Kill our enemies with guns and bombs.
- Help foreign governments improve instead of our own country.
- Diplomacy, what is that?

STOP, AND THINK WHEN YOU VOTE.

Your Great Grandmother always told me "you should not talk about someone after they have passed away, they will be judged where they are going". Although I have tried to live by this advice, there is so much forgotten, willingly or otherwise, about the Ronald Reagan story, that I feel you and all Americans, should not be deceived, when Ronald Reagan's legacy is being elevated to sainthood. Republicans want to bask in the sunset of Ronald Reagan's popularity.

This will be what I remember as the truth, not a myth. President Reagan's legacy is not as rosy as the Republicans would like you to believe. His stated goals as President;

- lower taxes,
- industry deregulation,

- and peace through strength.

Were those great ideas? If they were real but, you can be the judge. He did lower taxes, for the rich, from 50% to 28%, he certainly kept his word to his big supporters. At the same time he raised taxes on low-income workers. So for the first time in America's history, taxes for the rich were lowered while taxes for the workers were raised. Very Reaganesque. He also removed many of the poor from the tax rolls, a rare positive Reagan step.

Deregulation led to a flood of company mergers, not good for consumers or the workers involved. It has resumed, unabated, for seven years with George Bush. We can see the results when heads of government agencies cannot even protect our children from those deadly toys from China. A perfect example of the Republican philosophy, let private industry rule. A dangerous rule, that also created our economic catastrophe of today. Peace through strength, military strength, achieved with large fiscal deficits. And no matter what the facts are, Republicans continuously call themselves the party that has FISCAL responsibility, an out an out LIE. Democrats cleaned up the fiscal mess.

A partial list of Republican "achievements" while President Reagan was their leader.

- Iran-Contra, a foreign policy calamity without precedent. Illegally selling missiles to Iran's Islamic Revolutionary Guard. A Presidential black mark.
- Lebanon 1982, an American disaster, a President Reagan fiasco.
- Savings and Loan collapse, may have also caused the 1987 stock market crash. Over 1000 savings and loan companies bankrupt.
- 1982, Worse decline in economy since great depression. Blamed it on the Democrats, the   economy recovered very quickly.
- Reaganomics, trickle down economics, tax cuts for corporations. Economic hocus pocus. Money for the rich.
- He set out to reduce Social Security benefits for seniors. It was rejected by Republicans and Democrats alike.

- A union president to union buster! An underhanded Presidential action against the air traffic controllers union, without any consideration for the safety of the traveling public or the affect on our working people.
- A major health threat, Aids, raising its ugly head. He said "it was like the measles, it will go away." He would not address the aids issue until his actor/friend Rock Hudson died from the disease.

We could go on for several pages, but these are enough to show the utter disregard of the truth politicians have. Republicans will tell you they are tough on terrorists, after they supply them arms to kill our soldiers. What nonsense. The Soviet Union imploded when their military spending could not be supported, dissolving the USSR and bringing down the Berlin wall. Reagan outspent the Soviet Union on defense, that helped in the fall of the USSR. Was that peace through strength?

"MR. GORBACHEV, TEAR DOWN THIS WALL",

the Berlin wall statement heard around the world. Twenty years later, a photo-op, made for political gain, the same reason by a different president, on an aircraft carrier in full uniform,

"MISSION ACOMPLISHED". Two Republican Presidents, the old one was a master of illusions, the new one a master of deceit. President Reagan was vehemently opposed to Communism. He was protective of the American way and considered the USSR and Communist China as MORTAL ENEMIES. He was totally correct. He did however, allow American capitalists to do business in China, with very strict guidelines. China's President Deng Xiaoping was taking a Communist country, 1.3 billion people living in miserable, hopeless poverty, into capitalism. Today there is not a semblance of business guidelines for people doing commerce with China, being used by the Bush administration, it is the "Wild West of Wall Street", where the average person will take their lumps while the fat cats rake in the dough, by the billions. During the Communist takeover of China, you would be killed if they believed you had ever had connections with a capitalist.

Do you remember how one of our Chinese friends told the story of this kind of tragedy with her grandfather, beaten to death, he was called a capitalist conspirator, because he had business connections outside China. What a wonderful government it is, receiving our technology, free of charge. The results of Deng Xiaoping's efforts are astonishing. Twenty years later you cannot buy anything Made In America,

everything is made in COMMUNIST China or elsewhere. Good job corporate America, your profits are sky high and our jobs are now in hands of a Communist Government!

American capitalists, supported by our Republican government, cannot resist this unlimited slave labor. We are "sleeping with the DEVIL", Communist China. American private enterprise has proven that they do not care about working people or the country that made them great.

THEY ARE TRAITORS TO OUR WORKERS AND TO ALL AMERICANS.

President Reagan would fire any government employee who assisted the communists obtain unauthorized manufacturing capabilities. And it would not be like George Bush, who only knows how to change his promises.

SERVICE JOBS.

President Reagan talking about jobs, "service will be our most important job source", or words to that effect. WHAT? We are throwing in the towel? To hell with the workers of America, we cannot continue on our history of being the most vibrant and well-trained workforce in the world? Does anyone remember? Number one in technology, limited to service type jobs? DUH. Please, I do not want to demeanor service jobs, hard working people that are mostly underpaid, but how many living wage jobs can a service economy support? Does that mean that we can "create" jobs in the service sector and grow our economy? It sounded like we were on the road to a perpetual money machine. What movie do you suppose he learned that from?

A Republican Ronald Reagan myth.

Like we have today, not a word about a new training initiative for displaced workers, using new technologies to create jobs, solving our energy crisis, medical crisis, transportation, education, or any number of areas that required leadership and intelligence to recognize problems. Yes, we had all of the same problems 20 years ago. Understanding difficult problems was not one of Ronnie's strong suits. Did George Bush follow in his footsteps, by not understanding or thoroughly considering the gravity of starting a WAR? Many people intimated that he never considers Facts when making decisions, we now see it is true. Never let the facts cause you to change your mind, great thinking.

Where was the leadership needed to address the myriad of problems facing Ronnie?

Missing in action, a Ronald Reagan quality. Reagan started the process of decimating our working class in America, with the same Republican policies that have destroyed the living wage. And we want or need another President like Ronald Reagan?

NOT IN MY LIFETIME!

RONALD'S IRAN CONTRA SELLING MISSILES TO THE TERRORIST STATE OF IRAN!

For use by the Iranian Revolutionary Guard, (the same military organization that President Bush wants to declare war on) Committing a CRIME of great magnitude. It had consequences felt throughout the International community. When he is caught, Reagan proclaims it was an "arms for hostage" deal, referring to the American hostages who were being held by Iran. A few months later he admits He LIED, It was NOT. Many of the Presidents men, directly involved in this international crime, were indicted and some were convicted. Is that another trait inherited by our present President Bush? BREAKING THE LAW!

But not to worry, another Bush President, George H.W. Bush would soon arrive on the scene, to pardon those bad boys. After all, it was for our Security, wasn't it?

A REPUBLICAN/REAGAN MYTH, we are the LAW AND ORDER party.

Today we are having another re-run,
- The script, WAR and "terrorist" countries,

- above the law,
- break the law,
- deceive and lie,
- pardon - by the same family, different middle initials.

What a coincidence! Law and Order Republicans! SAY WHAT? There are few people who will challenge the exaggerations and lies of politicians when they use a deceased, respected President of the USA, as their protector. A typical Republican strategy is to lie, to convince voters a little poison will not kill them. Use constant commercial messages, with money provided by the fat cats, and many people believe them. What a way to get votes. America does not want another President that is like Ronald Reagan , who was more MYTH than substance.

RONALD'S IMMIGRATION POLICY .

Our present day un-solvable problem. Same problem in 1986 as in 2007, too many illegal's. Reagan signed the Immigration Reform Act where employers are REQUIRED, by Federal law, to check employee immigration status. Three(3) million illegal aliens were granted AMNESTY. Part of Reagan's speech on illegal aliens;

"these men and women will now be able to come out into the sunlight, they can become American citizens." Does it sound familiar to present day rhetoric? Are they also the same writers?

RONALD, THE UNION MAN

As an actor he was a Union Man, President of the Actors Union. As the Republican President of the United States of America, he becomes a Union Buster.

An oxymoron: A Republican Union Man

When the air traffic controllers went on strike in August, 1981, the President took control. They were warned, he gave them an ultimatum, forget your demands, go back to work or be fired. They didn't go back to work, they believed they had just cause to be on strike. He fired all 11,000 of them, no matter how important or real their claims were, or how important their jobs were to the safety of the American traveling public. He was the boss.

Is there any parallel to our present Republican President, who will do anything to show who is boss? A sad day for unions, a great day for the Republican party. And can you believe we still have some unions supporting the GOP? Republicans and our corporations, are every unions biggest adversary. Why would any union support, or even recognize that they exist, a Republican for public office? Deep Republican pockets?

Corrupt union leadership? Or an overwhelming supply of bogus information by politicians?

RONALD'S TRICKLE-DOWN ECONOMICS

President Ronald Reagan and his trickle down economics, with the rich getting a huge tax break while increasing taxes for the workers, firing government workers, decreasing spending for social programs(a Republican standard), significantly increasing military spending, all combined to create an economic downturn.

How does the second Republican helping taste? Some more? Anyone? As a result of Reaganomics, and the massive deficit he created, the United States went from the world's largest creditor nation, people lending money, to the largest debtor nation, those borrowing money, all on President Reagan's WATCH. Make sure we do not elect those "tax and spend Democrats, no fiscal responsibility," we hear it over and over,

MORE REPUBLICAN/REAGAN MYTHS.
Everyone, you better Wake up.
Democrats, that includes you.

Don't worry Republicans, a new disaster is in the works, you know, the Iraq thing. It will make poor Ronnie's deficit "look like an ant compared to an elephant."

A Republican legacy, OUTSPENDING the Democrats, will be saved.

Another Republican Myth, CONSERVATIVE Republicans.

What part of rhetoric do the American people not understand? Republicans do a great job with the crafty deception of "acting conservative", they are following Ronnie's act. Twenty years later Reagan's style of government, an incompetent attempt at leading our country, is being repeated today by George Bush and his administration. Give your money to the rich so everyone else will get a trickle. A trickle, that is nothing more than a drop, when it gets to the poor.

Another UP SIDE DOWN Republican story. Steal from the poor and give it to the rich. Did Ronnie ever play the part of Robin Hood in a movie? He often thought most of his actions were connected to some movie. As usual, the results are opposite of the real story, that is not much different than most politics, I guess. Ronald Reagan and the Republican politicians dug a deep hole for the American worker twenty years ago. George Bush and his administration have made it a crater. The average person will not survive the latest debacle if they have to work for a living and provide for a family. They have made it impossible, but they still do not recognize the need for any programs to help displaced workers. Is that a Republican attribute we can afford to mimic? Are the Republican candidates telling us, over and over, they want more of the same?

A Republican/Bush myth, THE ECONOMY IS FINE!

RONALD, THE LEADER.

Ronald Reagan is being portrayed as a man of great leadership and vision. A Washington Post story in the 1980's about President Reagan. "It is evident that most of the decisions being made in the White House are being made by President Reagan's staff and his wife." End of story. Of course that was after Nancy consulted with her personal astrologer, maybe the astrologer was the real decision maker.

What ASTROLOGISTS do the Republicans have lined up?

President Reagan was unable or unwilling to study intricate or difficult problems, ones that he was supposed to understand. His aids used cartoons to help him comprehend what was going on. A throwback to his acting days perhaps.

Have the Republican candidates signed any CARTOONISTS yet?

RONALD ON LEBANON.

Against all military advice (the kind President Bush argues is the only advice he needs, besides GOD) Reagan kept the Marines in Beirut. Devastating results, the barracks were bombed by terrorists, with hundreds of marines killed and injured. Of course the Republicans refer to this as a problem not addressed by the Democrats.

Still another Republican/Reagan MYTH.

If the Republican candidates want to be Reaganesque(heaven forbid, and they do) what should they be telling us? How about the TRUTH! It cannot be they want fiscal responsibility, can it? They have supported a Republican President who does not know what the word responsibility means, in any way, shape or form, much less put fiscal in front of it. How about being a Republican conservative? Is there any end to the hypocrisy they are willing to spew forth?

More Republican MYTHS.

REPUBLICAN FAMILY VALUES.

We have Republicans who state they want to "strengthen the family." Do they expect to do this by voting NO on all major legislation that,

- Supports children's health,
- Supports a living wage for the head of a household,
- Supports preventative healthcare for all,
- Supports the working persons right to join a union,

Strengthen Family Values, one more Republican MYTH.

Working for Minimum Wage, is that a joke? A family person with two children and another living on a minimum wage. Republicans(and some Democrats), force millions of Americans to live below the poverty level. And that's no joke!

Reform, who needs reform? You must one of those socialists or communists. Come on in, the economy is great! What! No money to invest? Sorry, you do not belong, try another time. We have seen 7 years of Republican NO votes, for programs that would improve the lives of millions of workers. A reminder, when are the Republicans going to realize, that we need a strong working class in America to prosper, not people in poverty, where capitalists like to keep all workers. It will not change any Republican persons mind knowing unscrupulous capitalists are decimating American families, they will still vote Republican. Republican candidates proclaim from the high stage of hypocrisy, that they are going to "strengthen" American families. But have they ever voted for any significant important social changes? NEVER.

Their record clearly shows what should be obvious to everyone. They are NOT for family values. Negative ads of political campaigns are designed to confuse and divide the voters. Money ends up as the biggest factor to win an election to public office, it buys the most negative ads that destroys your opponent. Many of these ads are even un-American. Unfortunately, in America, hundreds of millions of dollars in advertising will change people's minds, and produce votes. It would be great if someone could be elected, to public office, on their own positive positions, without millions of dollars for campaigning, and not trying to wreck the character of their opponent. Maybe some day we can make it happen.

Republicans continue to take care of the rich at any cost, Democrats play dead.

All Americans, must "take the bull by the horns" and straighten out this political mess.

MYTHS about President Ronald Reagan are Republican fairy tails, adopted by all faithful Republican politicians, to influence credulous voters.

And so much for our Republicans who want to be Reaganesque.

To my children:

Many young people of today do not even know who Ronald Reagan was, or what he did or did not do, as president. They certainly will NOT find him in the annals of GREAT presidents. But they will find him in many biographies, some that are very harsh on his actions or more correctly, his inactions as President. Republicans keep talking about him as the Great Republican Savior, and he may have been for them. He may have saved them from extinction, not by being a great leader, but by being an actor. President Reagan pretended(he always liked to act) that he was for the people, a typical Republican charade.

Republicans do not have enough votes in America to win any national election. Not without the help of smoke and mirrors to divide and conquer the popular vote, and enough money to challenge Bill Gates on a corporate spending spree. Shame on us and all Democrats for allowing this deceit to go unchecked.

Your Great Grandmother or Great Grandfather, as workers who knew the difference between a Democrat and a Republican, would wash my mouth out with soap for saying,
"I WANT TO BE LIKE RONALD REAGAN."
Yes - even if I am 75 years old.

Love our children, be happy and be kind;

Love
Dad/Grandpa
XXXXXXXXXX X2

LETTER 5

HEALTHCARE

PRIVATE ENTERPRISE
OR GOVERNMENT CONTROL

Hi everyone;

The healthcare debate is starting to simmer, we have elections coming and this is always a major topic, one that may make or break a candidate. What does America want to provide as their model for the future of healthcare? Everybody talks about it, no real solutions. Today, our healthcare system is UP SIDE DOWN, like all the issues I am writing to you about.

America is at a crossroads, everything we have "taken for granted" for the past 50 years, has changed. We were the best at almost everything in the world. If we were not, then we would make every effort to become the best. Healthcare is no exception.

Great medical advances were either developed here, or brought here and made a part of our healthcare system. Our doctors and medical scientists are among the best in the world. Our medical engineers and developers produce equipment that allows us to see inside the body, we can predict who will be at risk for certain diseases, how to replace body parts and repair severely damaged ones. When cured we are as good as "new". We have solved many of the mysteries of medicine, and we continue to do so. But we cannot find a way to have healthcare for EVERYONE in this great country. It is a disgrace for our society, regardless of who is in charge, Democrat, Republican or Independent. And that may be part of the problem, what should healthcare for Americans have to do with party affiliation?

Well it turns out that political parties have very much to do with healthcare, and with our very quality and length of life. If we provide everything for some, and nothing for those in need, we will in fact fit in the Republican Pro Life category, where most "conservatives" claim to be today,

VEHEMENTLY OPPOSED to good healthcare for a longer life and better quality of life, for EVERYONE.

It had been standard procedure in the past, that doctors were the kings, they reigned supreme over the life and death of most people. Now the insurance companies are playing with our lives. A file clerk, deciding without so much as an instant of hesitation, if you deserve to have life saving treatment.

The FORM says "you can live another day",

or the FORM says "you are going to die".

It's the FORM, everything is checked against you, we cannot prevent you from dying. Doctor's opinions are not needed, it is NOT covered.

No reprieve from DEATH ROW.

Any last wishes?

Sad to say but it is true, it happens every day with our up side down medical system.

Is this the system our politicians and our Republican friends are saying will provide the best for America? Is this the best private enterprise can do, nothing better? It must be time to leave America, maybe I will see where the doctors are going.

Oops, sorry, cannot afford to go there.

We need a major MEDICAL SYSTEM overhaul.

We need to redefine "healthcare providers", put the definition back to where it used to be. The word is providers, not withholders, it is not the IRS, but it is hard to tell the difference. You, private enterprise, are supposed to supply us with healthcare. They spend more time on denying procedures, than they spend on approving them. Why? Every rejection is increased profit, nothing to do with health. Stories have been printed that they get bonuses for the most denials, but I refuse to believe we have gone so low that we could do that. A health provider or a health denier? This kind of chicanery has to stop.

We are talking about America, not a third world country, where people are bought and sold like sacks of grain.

What are pre-existing conditions? Are we used cars being fixed? You didn't tell me you had an accident before I gave you the quote to fix you. All bets are off. What's that you say? A major immoral loophole to avoid paying for a health procedure. If everyone had to be in perfect shape before they got health insurance, there would not be anyone insured, except the very young and the rich, who can buy anything. You did not tell them you had a headache, 6 months before it was discovered you had a brain tumor.

You cheated. NO COVERAGE.

What are the ramifications of denying life saving treatment, effectively letting the patient die? Is this procedure any different than letting a person die, by denying food and water to someone in their care? If that person is guilty of withholding the essentials for survival, they will be sent to prison. Why aren't the insurance companies culpable? They put people in jail for abusing animals - abusing, not killing, animals. Should our society allow this cruelty to HUMANS to continue? It is not believable that an animal can provoke more public sympathy, than a poor person dying, from the lack of money or health insurance to obtain medical treatment. What a bottomless hole our country has gone into, a moral crisis that religious leaders should be addressing, instead of politics.

Are the CEO's of the private healthcare providers guilty of manslaughter? They instruct their clerks to deny life saving treatment, for the sole purpose of increasing profits, does that fall into the criminal category? Or do we put it in the disingenuous Pro Life category?

All the time "our providers" deny coverage, healthcare premiums continue to go up at 4 or 5 times the rate of inflation. This has been happening for years. Healthcare is now as expensive as owning a home. It is common for premiums to cost over $1000 per month for a family plan, a direct result of the Republican 50 yard dash to deregulation. Do our insurance companies know what the minimum wage is? A person earning twice the minimum wage, will earn enough to pay for premiums, nothing left to live on. What's the purpose of having health insurance if it means you are going to starve to death? For 50 million Americans, your neighbors and mine, that are without any form of healthcare, they say "tough luck buddy."

A ridiculous position to put a working person in, say a cook, who gets up at four in the morning, to go to work, to cook your favorite meal, in your favorite restaurant, for the best price in town. Do they deserve affordable healthcare? NO? "Who cares, if he does not cook, we can get someone else, or go somewhere else. I have the money, they have no choice." Is this you, Mr. Compassionate Republican? You are determined, we do not give anyone, except the rich, something for nothing. A compassionate conservative Republican? No, a low life.

Premiums? Shouldn't they be linked to the cost of living? Or is our cost of living not the same as theirs? You got it, they are not the same. They have to keep corporate shareholders happy, they want returns of at least twice the cost of living, otherwise they are not making enough profit. No bonuses for the bosses, stock prices will not go up. But this is healthcare isn't it? Peoples health and quality of life, if not life itself. Profits before health? "Oh no, we give you everything you deserve, we charge a processing fee, we cannot do all this work for nothing. That's common sense." A new one payer, not for profit system is required, to stop this Republican/Capitalist debacle. Healthcare, as provided by insurance companies, has the opposite goals of working people, you and me. Insurance company goals;

Keep the premiums GOING UP,
Keep DENYING care and REDUCING coverage.

American people goals;
AFFORDABLE QUALITY Healthcare, for EVERYONE.

That is what you would expect from the best country in the world. The up side down world of medicine, in America, in the 21st century. What a mess.

We need to start a top to bottom transformation of healthcare, make healthcare out of bounds for politicians. Lets come together as Americans, for every social, scientific, and economic program we undertake. Our leaders have deserted the workers and our social systems are out of whack for the 21st century. A top social problem, how to establish a healthcare system that works to keep Americans healthy, is desperately needed. It will be a system for all people, and we will include the present people who deny healthcare for the poor, true compassionate actions. Our country cannot survive if we continue with the politics of greed and corruption. Our pathetic politicians, working with corrupt private industry, are controlling our health and indeed, our lives. Working people have to say, STOP, today. We need to TAKE BACK AMERICA! It is time to be HONEST, to tell only the truth, be prepared to sacrifice and ACT like Americans, work together!

Honesty should include answering the questions; Why America, the only standing superpower in the world, spends billions of dollars helping everyone around the globe, more billions for WAR and war machines, yet we do not think it is reasonable to provide the opportunity for all Americans, not just the rich, to have proper healthcare?

Honesty should include answering the question; Why our government allows insurance companies and doctors, to provide its people with second class medicine, while paying first class prices?

Honesty should include answering the question; Why our prescription drug laws were written by the drug companies, not by our representatives, their only job?

Honesty should be answering the question; Why is it we cannot buy drugs from other countries, but contaminated medicine imported by the drug companies is OK?

Honesty should be answering the question; Why our private industry medical insurance companies have no government oversight?

Honesty should be answering the question; Why we do not ban medical lobbyists from our capital?

Honesty should be answering the question; Why we allow medical liability insurance for doctors to cost hundreds of thousands of dollars, that we end up paying?

We will stop here. Lets try to look at some of the stumbling blocks to having quality healthcare for all Americans. As a start, we need to see why we are up side down.

- Healthcare is the cheapest when you prevent disease or disorders from happening in the first place. How about the earth shattering idea of doing preventative medicine. In addition to 20th century care, medicine for the 21st century!

- Our current system is morally bankrupt. We treat the LIVES of people differently, those with "good" insurance or who have money, will be provided every possibility to live. Those without insurance or money, will receive a DEATH SENTENCE, if they have life threatening medical problems. Private insurance companies have replaced doctors, when dealing with life saving medical treatment.

- Christian Right, Moral Majority, Compassionate Conservatives, do you see anything wrong with this picture? Or is everything OK, as long as I am OK?

Our system is economically bankrupt. We spend more for healthcare than other industrialized nations and receive less, much less, in return. It is the same old Republican song, let private enterprise do it, they can do it best. Healthcare in America, a private enterprise humiliating FAILURE. It ranks right up there with all the other private industries who have stolen and sold America, for the almighty dollar. Healthcare, without government oversight, has proven to be catastrophic for everyone except the insurance companies.

Doctors leave their practice, not able to function as doctors, with the blanket of deception about proper patient treatment, created by the insurance companies. Insurance liability premiums of $100's of thousands, drive many doctors from their practice. Doctors prescribe a drug, it is sent to the insurance company to fill, it is rejected, too expensive. Who says it is too expensive, another doctor at the insurance company? No, the clerk receiving the order in the mail or fax, they check it on their list, reject it whenever possible. A doctors orders, overridden by a file clerk! Try that trick 50 years ago. Negative medical treatment, not providing the more expensive drug is more profit for the company, the bottom line is all that counts. We have the same situation in every medical case being processed by our "healthcare provider." Provide as little as possible, patient be damned, they have no where else to go, period.

Start using PREVENTIVE medicine practices today. We need to promote healthy lifestyles, provide incentives for those who maintain good health and pass laws eliminating many known health hazards. A good example, cigarettes. We had a great victory when the tobacco companies lost the class action suit against them. Or did we?

Claims of billions of dollars were settled in favor of the consumer. A paltry amount compared to the healthcare costs tobacco causes, and they will continue to escalate.

Who were the real winners? The TOBACCO companies! We did not stop the production and sale of tobacco. Not even one suggestion that these companies stop growing and producing tobacco products in America. We do not allow coca, marijuana, or poppy plants to be grown, because they will eventually kill people. We must not allow this destruction of human life to continue, ban it like we do other things that are deadly to everyone.

And they still target the selling of these cancer sticks to our young people, even pre-teens, so they will be addicted to nicotine for life. Statistics show that if kids can reach their twenties without being addicted to nicotine, they will have a great chance of never using tobacco products. That thought alone is worth outlawing cigarettes. We should re-double our efforts to prevent young people from smoking, yes, even at taxpayer expense. There is a lot of truth in the old saying, " an ounce of prevention is worth a pound of cure." We can use this saying to everyone's advantage. Do not allow the sale of cigarettes to anyone under the age of 30. That would be a starter while we put the tobacco companies out of business. It may be hard or impossible for many to quit smoking. If we ban tobacco today and invest in helping those people lick the addiction of nicotine, we will have scored a knockout for America. The long term payoff is enormous, it is the largest single item we need to conquer in our quest for universal healthcare.

Millions of people are still getting sick and dying, because of tobacco products. Who pays for these illnesses when smokers develop lung and heart problems? How much does tobacco contribute to our out of control health care costs? Are these same people who consume tobacco products, the ones who oppose universal healthcare? There must be some of them in that bunch. Tobacco is a path to self destruction. Tobacco companies know how to addict people to nicotine, but do not care about the diseases caused by smoking. They advertise that their products may be deadly, so why don't they just stop producing them? GREED!

Our government and private enterprise(tobacco companies), another example of capitalism that has turned deadly for Americans. Are there any other consumer products, that you put in your mouth, that contain a warning, "this product will cause death when used"? It may not be today, but it will get you. We ban many pollutants from being discharged into the air by power companies, chemical factories and other corporations. Yet we allow cigarettes to be sold, that contain the same harmful chemicals. People can ingest more toxins in a year with smoking, than you would receive by breathing air of most natural settings, in a lifetime.

At one time in our history, long before it was public knowledge that smoking will kill you, not may, but WILL kill you, tobacco companies were deemed necessary for the taxes that were collected from the sale of cigarettes. We now have all the information needed to say that was a stupid, senseless, destructive mistake, beyond belief. We are now paying heavily, we will pay more in the future in costs to everyone, and we will have a reduced quality of life for many. Even second hand smoke has proven to be a killer, of the innocent bystanders. For the millions of people who have smoked themselves into poor health, it will be a difficult road ahead. Cigarettes should be BANNED from America and the world.

HEALTHCARE PREMIUMS.

Who is on the side of the workers who make barely enough to live on, much less pay for healthcare premiums? Where are the spokespersons for the poor and the workers? Are there any provisions for a sliding scale premium, where what you pay is based on what you earn? "What, this is private industry, we have our stock prices to maintain, they come before healthcare. We give them back most of what they put in, can a government program beat that?" What should a worker do?

- Get another job, President Bush says the economy is doing the best in years, there are plenty of jobs. YOU already work two jobs?
- Get your wife a job, two pays may get some help. Your 12 year old can do something, can't he?
- Get a job where your employer provides healthcare insurance. WHAT? That has gone the way of living wages, defined benefit pension programs, company-worker loyalty, and job security.

Well we are sure of one thing, if private enterprise continues providing healthcare to American workers, at the present rate of premium increases, no one who works for a living will be able to afford it. An alternative must be found, damn the Republicans and the doomsayers who predict our healthcare will become much worse. The people saying that are usually the people that have adequate healthcare, at someone else's expense. It cannot get worse, if they deny care, increase premiums at will, and you cannot even afford to participate.

We need a national healthcare system, NOT FOR PROFIT, ONE PAYER, EQUAL CARE for all.

We need to talk about those who cannot afford premiums, but absolutely need to have healthcare to survive, live another day. He or she is without insurance, needs an MRI, so they have to pay for it themselves. They will be charged 2 or 3 times more than the insurance companies would pay, for the same test. Why? The insurance companies control healthcare, a steep discount price for me, you pay the "full list price," 10's of thousands of dollars at the end of an uncomplicated problem. Another burden on the less fortunate, those who can not afford to pay for premiums, much less a bill of tens of thousands of dollars. That is one of the reasons healthcare is the number one cause of

personal bankruptcy in America.

We were the richest nation in the world, but we could not provide basic healthcare for everyone. That makes us the most SELFISH nation in the world, by anyone's standards. We have gone from the UGLY American of 30 years ago, to the ME FIRST American of today, and with attitudes like we have, how we treat human beings, everywhere, it is no wonder we have a very negative reputation in other countries.

- For Christians it is a sin against mankind.
- Religious Right Republicans, take note. A SIN.
- Can you go to Heaven if you do not obey the Bible?
- Isn't denying someone life saving care, IMMORAL?
- Or is disregard for human life, when it is for profit, not a sin?

Republicans read from the Republican Bible, Bush Edition,

"Love thy neighbor, except the poor".

Should our government be monitoring private enterprise when they supply services that are a monopoly, or provide something essential for life? It was that way when I was young and America was a Democracy. Electric power, telephone service, public water supplies, medical providers, were all regulated by the government, either federal or local, to prevent excess profits. It protected the average citizen. Now we have stripped every regulatory law from the books, or we have stripped every regulatory agency of their independent inspectors, and installed political hacks, appointed by our political whacks. Remember when President Bush praised one of his "best" appointments, Brown, to head up our Homeland Security Department? Browns previous experience was raising Arabian horses. Was he a friend of Prince Bandar, who Bush used as his foreign affairs advisor? When Hurricane Katrina hit New Orleans, Brown didn't even know what was happening. His department was responsible for providing assistance to the thousands of people in harms way. They were dying, left for days sitting on roof tops, trapped in their homes, in their attics, trying to survive. Where was Brown?

Out to lunch!

The biggest fiasco of its kind in American history. Then remember President Bush praising him, "Good job Brownie". It probably was a good job, for someone who didn't have the foggiest idea about what he was supposed to do or how to do it. What an appointment for our Homeland Security department. Just think if we had a security problem, the terrorists would be running our country in a matter of days. An appointment to run a MAJOR Federal Agency, without any qualifications whatsoever? What a discouraging look into our government "leader qualifications" and their backgrounds.

Can you visualize what kind of qualifications President Bush's other important appointments have. Most are not as evident as Homeland Security, but look at another very apparent attempt to "stack the deck". Nominating his secretary to be on the Supreme Court. What an insult to the Supreme Court and the American people. If his other appointments compare to the choices of Brown and Harriet, it is no wonder we have such a hopeless government.

We no longer have any oversight for most healthcare providers, because we know private enterprise will provide the best solution. WRONG. WRONG. WRONG. It was in the 1980's that another Republican President, Ronald Reagan, had industry de-regulation as one of his main goals and it looks like he did a good job. It is very sad to say, but deregulation has crippled America's chances to provide healthcare for all. We will never overcome the healthcare deniers, there are THREE(3) TRILLION dollars at stake, how hard are they going to fight for that.

An article about healthcare.

Forbes Magazine, September 17, 2007 issue, page 117.

The 16th most powerful WOMAN in the WORLD.

She is Angela Braly, CEO of WellPoint, the health insurance company that has 34 million members, and controls a huge amount of the healthcare money in the United States.

Article highlight - WellPoint's earnings have risen 55% a year, on average since 2000, to $3 BILLION a year. End of highlight. Earnings, it goes next to the word profit, 55% - imagine - 55%, not for one year which could be an anomaly, but for 7 consecutive years.

It sounds more like the inflation rate of a third word country, not the earnings of a health insurance company in America. One half of the WellPoint profit comes from premium INCREASES, you know, what you see reducing your paycheck every month. As a believer in the American Way and private enterprise, it is depressing, to say the least, that American companies are allowed to make exorbitant profits on the backs of American workers, for healthcare. We are talking about healthcare, not a dispensable item, where people can charge what they want, 55% profit may be small change for some commodities.

WellPoint has grown to where it has a major portion of the U.S. healthcare market. Through acquisitions, including bringing not-for-profit groups into the for-profit WellPoint corporate structure, at taxpayers expense, and premium increases of 10% to 20% per year, Angela Braly has created a company that makes outlandish profits, for stockholders and herself, by controlling who gets healthcare and how much it will cost.

What a way to run healthcare in America. It is a good thing all healthcare deniers do not follow in her footsteps. Unfortunately, many are certainly trying.

With Braly leading the way, WellPoint started a $2,000,000.00 campaign, against the Governor of California, Arnold Schwarzenegger. The Governor plans to try to help all the people of California obtain healthcare, something private enterprise is determined to PREVENT. Is this a demonstration of America's way of using "private enterprise" to improve healthcare for everyone? They are going to run ads, comparing the Governor's efforts to provide healthcare for everyone in California, to electricity blackouts in their state." Say what? Everyone on the planet knows the primary cause of the California blackouts was GREED. Using white collar crime and corruption, energy companies were manipulating the market to make more profit, what she does legally. It was proven in court, company executives are still in jail today for their criminal activity.

Angela may be the 16th most powerful women in the world, but it's the NEW WORLD economy, where Communist China leads the pack, good company for her. The Communists have the same compassion, a few thousand less lives is good for their country, they have too many people. Bad news for America, UNREGULATED private enterprise has taken over. Angela Braly says; "We have to be disciplinarians about cost and quality". Every cost except hers. What used to be called "price gouging", is her highest quality. Our medical premiums have gone through the roof. We have ourselves to blame for this miscarriage of healthcare, we do not DEMAND oversight. No other industry, except oil, has seen costs go up unrestricted, out of control, like our medical system.

When WellPoint throws in statements that "we have to make people ACCOUNTABLE", we need to wonder what they mean. Is it the corporate chiefs who deny healthcare, making them "accountable" for someone's death? Or is it the company president that makes millions of dollars in salary, but cannot provide healthcare for their workers? Are the corporate owners accountable? Maybe she could help a poor person with some crumbs from her multi-million dollar bonus.

In the Forbes article they cite bonuses to hospitals and doctors, $140 MILLION in 2006, to "improve results". Does that mean patients have better care, their health is improved compared to other hospitals, that they have better doctors and nurses? I wish.

It is for those who saved her company money, secondary to healthcare quality.

Medical LIABILITY LAWS must be changed. Why are liability insurance premiums so high for doctors? You could compare it to the Catholic Church. The church was faced with pedophile priests, and the bosses moved them from one parish to another, only to commit their heinous crimes over and over. Doctors refuse to stop known PROBLEM doctors, they belong to the unspoken medical union, they have special "rights". When they become a financial problem, they tell them to "find another place to practice." Will they inform anyone else of the dysfunctional doctor? NO! A sure recipe for disaster, for patients, not the doctor. Like the bad priests, BAD DOCTORS continue to ruin peoples lives. The medical union must be broken, so this chain of events will also be broken.

There is an understood union for doctors practicing medicine, and it extends to the medical schools that train them. If your father or grandfather graduates from med school, you will get into med school. Well qualified students, those who are in the top 10% of their class, apply to medical schools. Many of these well qualified students are not allowed to become MD's, but we bring doctors in from all over the world with credentials that may not measure up to American standards. What is it that I do not understand about how we operate our medical education system? America's medical school admissions need to be doubled, new medical schools started and opened to all who qualify, not just the elite. It is not different than any other union, if your family is in, you get in. Others, forget about it, except for a token few. We spend close to $3.0 trillion, $3,000,000,000,000.00, on healthcare per year, that's more than $6000.00 for every man, women and child in the United States. You mean the brightest people on the planet, medical doctors, cannot put together a system that covers everyone and gives quality care with that amount of money?

Come on, Doc, give me a break.

Doctors have kowtowed to medical insurance companies and allowed private enterprise to do the opposite of what it is supposed to do. They should present the most efficient way to provide medical care, but they are a dismal failure. The problem is simple and already stated, America's goal is the best medical care, for our money, for everyone, that can be provided, the medical industry has a different goal, keep as much of the medical dollar being spent, for themselves, end of story. Seems we have private enterprise utterly opposed to what we need in America, affordable, quality healthcare for all. Where is the oversight to prevent this from happening? Republican? Democrat? President? Anyone? And the Republicans see no reason to change, "the private sector will do what's best for America." What they should say is "they DO America best", that would be closer to real life.

The Democrats are talking about using the existing healthcare structure, the present insurance providers, to collect the $3.0 trillion and let them distribute it their way.

A thousand foxes to guard the hen house. What an out and out blunder! Democrats, smarten up! It sounds like the same kind of thing we are seeing everywhere these days, private enterprise, screwing the common person. Private enterprise under the Bush Administration is out of control, they are not looking out for what's best for America and the worker is paying the price.

Back to Angela Braly for a moment. Besides being outrageous as to how they achieve their wealth, her comment in this article, about China's healthcare, was telling.

"In China they roll you out of the hospital if you run out of cash." Has communist/capitalist China already succumbed to the greed and power of the capitalists, removing the ONLY good thing that Communism actually provides,

FREE medical care for all. That is a major catastrophe for the Chinese people. They will need vastly improved healthcare services when the results of their uncontrolled pollution takes effect.

If a Chinese peasant needs cash to get into a hospital, they will die long before they are admitted. Chinese workers were at the top of the heap if they made $50.00 a month in the 1980's. Wages have changed enormously in the last 20 years, now many compare to workers worldwide. But that is for millions of manufacturing workers, not for most of the 1.3 billion people in Communist China. How much cash do you think a peasant could accumulate living on the equivalent of a few dollars a day? She must be looking at the new capitalist/Communists in China, where a few will achieve enough to pay for healthcare. Perhaps she could do something for the Chinese government, they are quite adept at deception and denying things a person needs to sustain life, when it serves their purpose.

Yes, she is right about being "rolled out of the hospital". It was a common sight, near the main City of Shanghai hospital, to see a person being rolled down the street on a hospital gurney. The reality was that they were DEAD, being wheeled down the street,

to the crematorium. What state of insincerity are we coming to? A new world of information and communication should put an end to such nonsense. "What do I care about this CEO and her comments, she is no different than any other CEO," you say.

If this woman, with a tremendous influence on our healthcare costs at the national level,

considers it negative for healthcare providers to role you out of the hospital if you do not have money, she should look at America and the policies she uses, where they do exactly the same thing. It happens every day, in America, all in the name of Angela's corporate profits, the only measure of success capitalists use for healthcare. Does that make her the 16th most powerful HYPOCRITICAL woman in the world? Or is good healthcare for all, not important?

A side note on healthcare in China. While in Shanghai, I needed a growth removed from my finger. It was getting to be a problem and I did not want to wait until my next trip back to the USA. One of our plant supervisors volunteered to introduce me to a surgeon at the local hospital. Believe me, a Chinese hospital is not someplace you want to be, for anything. The surgeon spoke very good English, looked at the finger and said no problem.

We set up a time, he had the operating room prepared and he removed the growth. It was in fact without a problem, except that the nurse had to keep banging the cauterizing machine, with her fist, to make it work. We got thru it. The doctor sent the growth to the lab to make sure it was not malignant. Later he informed me it was OK. And then the BIG SURPRISE! He presented me with the bill, $10 US, or 40 Yuan, for all the costs. Can you imagine, $10.00, for the doctor, nurse, lab and hospital fees. We are not talking about 100 years ago, this was China in 1986.

Another tidbit about the medical profession in China. Medical Doctors, yes MD's are(were) the lowest paid workers in China. This tells you something of the value the Chinese put on an individuals life, nothing. At one point while working in China, I had a young lady secretary who was a medical doctor. She made 2 times more money being a secretary than she was paid by the government as a doctor.

Just one more fact. While medical care was free in China, that does not mean that it is any different than it is in the United States of America. Our Chinese housekeeper had a 3 year old daughter that could not walk. She needed an operation that would correct a congenital abnormality. Our housekeeper had been trying for 2 years to get her child an operation, but although medical care was free, without "money or connections" she could not get it done. She needed the equivalent of $300.00 US to pay the surgeons(don't forget medical care was free) to perform the operation. At that time, it would take them more than 10 years to save enough for the operation, based on their salaries. In ten years it would be too late for the operation to correct the problem so we gave her $300, the operation was successful and the little girl could walk for the first time. This is an important story, not from the "we did something good" aspect of seeing the little girl walk for the first time, but because it demonstrates the depth of our immoral treatment of the needy, everywhere. It is also important because it shows how money is more important than ethics, worldwide. Money, the world's only priority.

DOCTORS AND COMPUTERS.

At this time doctors use computers in everyday practice, to make sure you are on time for your appointment, and that you pay the bill. Some are now using computers to input patient info, some are even digitally integrating internal test results. But doctors are light years away from utilizing 21st century technology to integrate America's healthcare system. Are we worried about medical privacy issues? We have a national medical data bank that is used by the insurance companies, and for nefarious purposes. They have to determine who they can insure, people with previous medical problems are not allowed to purchase healthcare. It would not be good business practice to give a person insurance if they have pre-existing conditions. Oops, can't give her insurance, she had breast cancer. So it cannot be about privacy.

Fantastic gains have been made with computers that are used for diagnosis and treatment in the medical field, but integration of all the data covering a patient's treatment is sorely lacking, often leading to tragic results. We hear personal information is misplaced, sent to the wrong place, the wrong limb is removed, a healthy organ is removed instead of the one that is diseased, lab information is mixed up between patients,

the wrong medical dosage is given, in some hospitals more often than you would believe. All these problems could be significantly reduced if maximum use of computers and technology were fully utilized, but the security and well being of the patient is secondary to the "is it cost effective" routine for the doctor and his practice. A transformation of the doctor/patient examination procedures needs to be implemented.

We have technology available that can transform the doctor - patient discourse and achieve better, quicker, more accurate results. It would free the doctor to do more evaluation for a given problem and spend less time, reducing costs. Wellness tests should be done when you are healthy, starting at an early age, before any problems arise. That information should be digitally stored as a patients "carry in to the doctors' appointment" information. Every doctor the patient visits must be recorded, the diagnosis entered and the treatment regime with all drugs prescribed, permanently recorded. NO exceptions. It would be part of the new PREVENTION program. A secure World Wide Web and Internet link can provide instant access to specialists in every medical field, including international connections as well as national. Radiologists in India are already being used to analyze CAT scans for USA medical facilities(who would have though we would be outsourcing medical doctors). Healthcare professionals from all fields will be utilized. We have a hodgepodge of treatment techniques that need to be synchronized, to best use our scarce and expensive medical facilities.

In this small area in Florida with about half a million people, we have 6 hospitals with public access to all, and a hundred specialized medical facilities, for private use. Private facilities that are built, equipped, and staffed by doctors, who endeavor to skirt the Medicare laws, insurance company rules and the strict guidelines needed for full service hospitals. That way they can get a bigger chunk of the healthcare pie. These facilities are usually owned by the doctors who have invested their time and money, but there are often many for the same medical procedures and they are underused, resulting in higher costs to the healthcare system. Doctors, like all other Americans, will have to learn, that what is best for the individual, may not be best for America. We need to work together, patient, doctors and all healthcare providers.

There are many healthcare professionals who are not allowed, some by questionable laws, to use the skills they have been trained to do. They may infringe on the "turf" of what doctors consider reserved for themselves. That period of medical practice has to come to an end. Pharmacists should be able to dispense medicine like they are trained to do, not count pills. They should assume responsibility of drug reactions and interaction with all the patients' drugs. With our "one record for all doctors" approach, everything is recorded and cross checked for potential interaction problems. Therapists should treat sprains and muscle aches without the patient first seeing a doctor(just so they can write a prescription), chiropractic and acupuncture should become a standard option when appropriate, drugs are not always the best answer. There are many other forms of alternative medicine that have proven to work, but fall outside the present day MD realm of practice. They need to be utilized.

It is essential, that when healthcare providers are dividing the healthcare pie, doctors and insurance companies have to put the patient first, not more profit. All doctors do not have right to become millionaires over night. This will be exceptionally hard for some physicians, who have egos that will not fit in the Superdome. A single payer not for profit system is needed. A "novel" system where the doctor makes the decision as to what is necessary, not an insurance company clerk.

My own actual experience to get a prescription refilled, it happened this way, maybe not blow by blow but close enough, it goes something like this; my doctor writes a prescription for a Yearly Renewal, the medicine I am renewing has been effective at treating the symptoms of my chronic disease. I have been taking this medicine for several years. The script is sent to the drug company that provides prescription service for the insurance company. The company, on a letterhead with a doctors signature, decides I should first try some other drug, they do not fill the prescription.

A letter from the drug company, "Please tell your doctor that you should try this other drug, its just as good and it costs less than what your doctor ordered." I call the drug company and ask to speak to a supervisor(already been through the clerk runaround). Who is the doctor at the drug company, I asked, that I could talk to about this change of my prescription? It says Dr. Smith on the letter, is he available, or could he return my call? What do you mean change of prescription, she answers, we just want you to use a drug that is just as good, it has a different name. But it is not a generic for what my doctor ordered, I stated. Well we now a have a tier system for drugs, you start out on the cheapest drugs, for your condition, and if that does not work, we can go to the next tier.

But I have been there, done that, I am not starting out, I explain. You have your doctor call us and we will explain that small detail to him. Well I need that medicine, I am almost out of the last order, I plead. Sorry, have the doctor call. Good by. Click.

A revolting dilemma our healthcare insurance companies have put the doctor and the patient in today. Insurance company selective coverage, even for those with good health insurance. Oh NO! A single payer system! You would be eliminating all those healthcare companies that are doing such a marvelous job. Can you imagine how many CEO's, CFO's, big time doctors, company presidents and vice presidents would be out of work? But not to worry, they all have golden parachutes, worth hundreds of millions of dollars of company proceeds. YOUR money. Put a not for profit corporation in charge of healthcare. Private enterprise has proven to be incompetent, incapable and callous while performing the task.

Last, but not least, we have to put medical liability lawyers out of business by improving our legal and medical systems. These liability lawyers, often conspire with others to help defraud the insurance companies. Another prestigious profession, lawyers, scrambling at the top of the money pile. Is it any wonder that doctors, and ultimately you , are paying $250,000.00 and $500,000.00 a year for liability insurance premiums? With the medical liability lawyers out of business and a one payer system, we would have a great start to national healthcare. It would open the door to 21st century medicine.

To My Children;

We have seen our healthcare system go from expensive to outrageous to unaffordable. Our children need better, we have to regain control of health care, private insurance companies and doctors have created an ignominy of national magnitude. Every industrialized country in the world, provides better healthcare, for all their citizens while we spend more and get less, much less.

Millions of dollars will be spent, to keep insurance companies in control of this huge medical conglomeration. We cannot let the bombardment of insurance company dishonest and deceitful TV ads, that use false information and FEAR tactics, sway out decisions. Healthcare needs a single payer system, run by a not for profit corporation, with strict government oversight and NO political meddling.

Stay healthy, be happy and be kind,

Love, Dad/Grandpa

XXXXXXXXXX X2

LETTER 6

SOCIAL SECURITY OR *PRIVATE ACCOUNTS*

Hi Everyone;

How the time flies when you are 70 something. It seems like yesterday that I sent the last letter. One of the latest comments of a presidential candidate, something to the effect that Social Security will be bankrupt before your generation is old enough to receive any benefits, reminds me of how we put SS into that state of insolvency. Over many years, everyone who has been involved with the Federal budget has raided the monies of SS, as if it was a cookie jar to be used when they were hungry for funds. Why doesn't the government use SS money to invest in the stock market, like they expect you to do when and IF they privatize SS? That of course would not be a prudent thing to do. You never really know what is going to happen with the stocks, with companies like Enron in the mix, or who will rip off many billions of dollars from the investments. The fact is they do not invest the SS money anywhere, it is too important a slush fund for Congress, to tie it up in investments.

Republicans would have you invest your own money, have no Social Security fund at all. Sounds great for the haves, not so good for the workers of America. If you think that the average person, who works for an hourly wage, will have the resources to determine how and where their retirement money should be invested, then you do not know Wall Street or the people who run it. It is questionable where the shadiest people are, Wall Street or Pennsylvania Avenue. It is for sure they are not out to protect OUR investments.

We need to look at the total pension system in our country if we are going to create a reasonable retirement solution for all. We have hundreds of retirement programs that operate independently throughout the country and many of them are supported by your taxes. For starters lets begin at the local level, your town or city government. You and your community, employ many people. You may not believe that or think you do not have anything to say about these employees, but you do. It is your taxes that will pay the wages and provide benefits for these employees. Even in the smallest of towns, elected officials, teachers, police officers, fire fighters, custodians, everyone who works for the town or city, may have a pension benefit that needs to be paid. The town, city or state has the responsibility to ensure their employee's retirement funds are provided and protected. They have a significant impact on the taxes you pay. Has your community provided for retirement contingencies in the current budget? Until a few years ago most towns or state agencies did not even consider the future impact of retirement costs in their budgets. New laws do address some of the potential costs, but if we are treated the same as in private industry, you had better hold on for a steep decline in retirement benefits.

There are some people that are still reaping great retirement rewards from you, via town, city and state governments, all over this country. They have worked for the benefits and they deserve to get them if that was what they were promised. The problem is that you have to foot the bill, with TAXES and if it is not properly planned it can be difficult for the taxpayers.

In 2007, a newspaper article about a firefighter, actually he was the fire chief, who was retiring. It was a relatively small community in Florida, the chief was a prominent person, hence the article. This example assumes the newspaper to be correct, I would like to believe it is not. The fire chief had 25 years of service with the community, his salary had reached $100,000.00 per year. When he retired his pension exceeded this salary while he was employed, he was now "entitled" to a yearly pension of over $100,005.00. There are not too many places where you can duplicate that. How is it possible that you can retire with more money than you made while employed, in a position paid by the taxpayers?

- Who will it be responding to MY emergency? You will not settle for anything but the best! The problem is that paying the most money does not necessarily get you the best of anything, including firefighters.
- Second, most firefighters belong to a UNION, they will usually have a reasonable salary, substantial benefits and as shown in this example, a great pension plan.
- Third, they will get paid as the union negotiates, normally based on what a firefighter receives in a comparable town or city elsewhere, not necessarily based on what the community can afford or they should have to pay.
- Fourth, during the last few years of employment, before retirement, they will work as much overtime as they can. This period, when their pay will be highest, will determine the basis for their retirement. In the case of the fire chief, I do not know if that $100,000.00 was his regular salary or a salary "adjusted" by other means, and there are many ways to tailor retirement for workers who are paid by taxpayer money.

Most fireman will retire long before they would if they had to depend on SS, by 10 years or more. If nothing else is taken into consideration, to retire that extra 10 years earlier than the normal retirement age of 65, with full pay, requires a retirement fund so large that very few people can even come close to acquiring that much money. Do firefighters automatically contribute 30% or more of their pay into a retirement fund when they become employed? If they can afford to do so, we must be paying them too much. Ordinary workers are required to pay their SS and have little left to save. This is not to criticize firefighters; they have a dangerous job to do and they do it well. If they are injured on the job or their health is affected, they should be fully compensated by the taxpayers, they were hired to protect them. But they cannot retire 10 or 20 years earlier than everyone else, with full pay. It will not work for the long run and it is unfair to the taxpayers.

It is a small cog in the big wheels that make up pension programs, so we have to look at everything. But consider this. Based on actuarial tables, this chief will collect his full salary in retirement, for around the same length of time that he worked as a firefighter. Seeing that his life expectancy at age 55 is about 82 years, he will collect for 27 years, almost $3 million. How much can a person of modest income, assuming he started with a nominal salary and did not always make $100,000, earn on his investments during the 25 years he was employed? It depends on how much he invests, what his employer contributes and his luck with the stock market. In this case a sizable fund of millions of dollars will be required when he reaches 55, especially if there is a cost of living provision included.

The question, who pays for these retirement programs? We do, mostly through our property taxes. Try to have a worker in the private sector get such a deal. That pension for the fire chief is 4 times (400%) more than what a person would receive from Social Security, after they reach the retirement age of 65, not age 55. This (city) employee will receive more benefits for 25 years of service, than what most people receive after 30, 40, or even 50 years of working and paying into SS. He will probable move on to another fire district to work in some capacity, and earn additional retirement benefits. It happens all the time. The new retirement age is approaching 67, where months or years are added to age 65, depending on when you were born. The fire chief was about 50 years old!

We argue about increasing the minimum wage for the lower level workers, many who do important jobs for our community. They have custodians and maintenance workers in the same city who are paid minimum wage, a level below poverty. This chief made ten(10) times the minimum wage. Is it reasonable for a firefighter to make 10 times the minimum wage and another worker to make the minimum wage, even if they have significantly difference jobs? Are they given special opportunities because of our FEAR, firefighters must be the best, and we cannot have minimum wage firefighters, can we?

A question about firefighters. When I was young, many towns had volunteer firefighters. They were from every level of the society, an auto mechanic to the mayor would answer the fire call, as volunteers. When the town grew, it required full time "fire men", that is what they were called before women became fire fighters. They usually received on the job training to become certified as a fireman.

How did the title of being a "professional" firefighter become the norm? As I remember the word it was reserved for people who were professionals, like doctors, lawyers and college professors. A person that gets on the job training to become "certified", was called a person of the trades, a technician or other suitable name.

A "professional" firefighter? Have they created a profession without prerequisites? Or is on the job training, at taxpayer expense, now considered enough to become a professional. I just hope my house does not catch on fire, they will have trouble finding my address.

We should look at another example of an employee that may be outside the umbrella of the SS system, TEACHERS. One of the most important assets we have in this country, bar none. There are 100's of pension plans that provide retirement funds for these underpaid professionals. It is impossible to say that this example applies to all, but many are like that being described. The value placed on the services of our teachers depends on the wealth of the community where they are teaching. A very wealthy suburb of a major city for instance, may find it reasonable to pay a high school teacher $100,000.00 per year. A teacher earning this amount per year could retire with $50,000 to $75,000 in annual benefits, not counting healthcare provisions.

An inner city or small town teacher with essentially the same credentials as the big city suburban teacher may earn one half that amount, many earn less than $50,000. It is supposed to be the cost of living in that locality, that makes such a discrepancy in salaries.

Their salaries are one half, so their pensions will be one half. We provide some people, like teachers, with better pensions, financed by teacher AND taxpayer money, while we talk about not supporting someone who barely survives on SS. Why?

- First and foremost, FEAR. We are afraid that if we do not provide the best for our children, they will not excel.
- Second, most teachers belong to a UNION.
- Third, they all perform one of the most important functions in our society, teaching our children.
- Fourth, they have college degrees that took four years of hard work and thousands of dollars to complete, to be "certified" as a teacher.

In earlier times teachers were grossly underpaid and they needed help, but they have gained ground when compared to present private enterprise salaries and benefits, they should no longer need subsidies. They often chose the life style that teaching provides or they are some of the few remaining patriots, willing and anxious to help children. Who pays the teacher salaries and provides the retirement benefits? YOU, your local school taxes(as well as state and federal taxes). YOU, the person that may one day have to live on SS benefits.

Let us look at another person who works in the sun, rain, snow or sleet, the MAILPERSON. He or she works for the Federal government or its quasi government brother, unless of course they're tied up in the infamous part time scenario.

- These workers also have a union.
- They will receive benefits as outlined in their defined pension program.
- They can receive 75% of their pay after 40 years of service. 40 years may sound like a long time, but when you think of it, all workers who start out in their 20's will have worked more than 40 years by the time they are at SS retirement age.

With 30 years service they can retire at age 55. Again, we see the amount received for a pension can be 2 to 3 times more than what they would receive if they worked under SS.

That is 200% to 300% more, not 20% or 30% that may be reasonable.

Let us look at one more example of how these retirement systems work, often to the detriment of the ordinary worker. A painter, who is like almost all service type persons who you rely on to make your life more enjoyable, or just plain easier. This painter works on his own, pays over 12% into the SS fund, about 6% as the employee and 6+% as the employer, plus his Medicare and other taxes. By working hard he earns enough to have a home and raise a family. If he is lucky and makes $75,000 per year, he can expect to receive SS benefits that are less than 25% of what he earned when painting, after he reaches retirement age of 65 to 67 The average SS monthly payment in 2006, was around $1000.

Can someone live on one fourth of what they made while they were gainfully employed? Not without drastic lifestyle changes, even then, maybe not. Most people who have a "regular" job and do not get some kind of special treatment concerning retirement,

will NEVER be able to retire. Millions of workers in America with "special programs," will retire with a reasonable income, 50% to 80% of what they were earning, a lot better than SS, at least until inflation or another disaster cause's havoc to their retirement plans.

Special retirement programs are made possible by employee contributions and with the taxes YOU pay for state and federal income tax, sales tax, personal and real estate and a myriad of other taxes. Contributions of the individual are a key part of the equation.

In most ordinary jobs where people are on their own, and workers do not have the opportunity to be part of a subsidized retirement program or have someone overlooking their investments, a private account loses a significant portion of its worth because of "fees" paid to the brokers, reducing the retirement value. The ordinary worker who puts in his 40 to 60 hours per week, will have no way to retire using SS, we need a different plan.

Without regard to anything I have already mentioned, most workers will never work for the same company long enough to retire, even if they did have a retirement program. With mergers and outsourcing, most companies have either gone to China, been absorbed by another company or they declared bankruptcy, long before an employee has worked there for 20 or 30 years. The first casualty in these cases is usually the pension plan, your hard earned savings for 10 or 15 years.

Hold on, "That's why we want to change to private accounts. SS is a burden on most workers." That is what President Bush says, it has proven to be a drastic error. With the volatile hedge fund market, on the WILD WEST of Wall Street, where the managers can make a billion dollars a year, yes, a billion dollars for managing a hedge fund, who is going to end up paying these enormous giveaways, the wretches of Wall Street? Not on your life, those wonderful private accounts, YOU, in another form, will foot the bill.

With what we once called "American" corporations, leaving our shores at a breakneck speed, and an administration that is oblivious of the threats to our workers losing their jobs any day, we need something that is definite for everyone's retirement.

Without profound changes, the uneven treatment of persons reaching retirement age will be a major obstacle to reform. Those are some of the "legitimate disparities" we see in America's retirement programs. We need to see what else is bringing SS down, into insolvency.

AN ILLEGAL WORK PRACTICE.

Lets look at the illegal practice of having individuals "work under the table", very common, given a blind eye by most people. That's where the employer pays the employee cash, sometimes barter, without deducting or paying taxes. They are usually hired by a small business that may be trying to avoid paying their fair share of taxes, they do not want the hassle involved with doing the right things, or cannot get it right if they try, necessary when you employ people for a business. It serves as a disincentive to those workers who should, but will not, pay their SS tax or Federal income tax. That money, for tax purposes, may not exist, either for the person hiring them or the worker. This illegal endeavor can give the dishonest employer a competitive advantage, their costs to do business are immediately much lower than an "above the table" legitimate employer. And the worker is getting more money per hour, because he is hiding his income. The IRS calls that stealing, it is illegal.

When these same workers get to be middle aged, they begin to think of retirement. They look for employment where they can pay into SS, they want to be eligible to collect SS benefits at age 65. Some workers have gone for 20 or 30 years without paying their share, a little more than 6% of their income, into SS. In addition, SS has lost the employers share of 6+%, for a loss of over 12% for those 20 or 30 years. When there are millions of people doing this, it becomes a serious burden on those who are trying to work by the rules, another example that shows it is not the fundamentals of SS that are bad, it is our society breaking the rules. It only takes 40 quarters(10 years) of legitimate employment to receive SS benefits at retirement age. We need to change that, with the exceptions of disability.

ILLEGALS

The previous examples are for the people who are American citizens. When you include the 10(20, 30?) million illegal aliens in our country, the fate of SS becomes even more grave. Many illegals will receive SS benefits and many will receive SSI. A lot should not qualify, but since SS and SSI are social SAFETY nets to help the unfortunate, they will. Throw in the rampant use of forged documents, and it becomes an even larger problem. Illegals are a drain on the SS system, mostly because they do not spend 30 or 40 years paying into the system before they collect benefits.

"Working under the table" and hiring illegals has been around since I can remember, they talked about it back around 1947, when I earned my first paycheck. That does not mitigate the fact that they cause a major drain on our society, especially SSI and most social help programs. These problems extend into all segments of our society and will probably be there for a long time to come.

CORPORATE RETIREMENT SYSTEMS

We need to look at the corporate system of providing retirement programs for their workers. When defined benefit programs are being used, it is common practice for large corporations to UNDERFUND employee retirement, often by millions or billions of dollars. There are new laws to prevent this but they are presently ineffective and will not be a factor for several years to come. Many of America's best know companies went bankrupt with under funded pension accounts.

British Petroleum(BP), you know, the company that changed their name to "Beyond Petroleum" in their advertisements to avoid being perceived as a foreign company, is a very large British oil company that absorbed several American oil companies, it has a pension plan that is presently billions of dollars under funded. They promised to pay for the retirement benefits of the employees, but they refuse to put up the money to fund the programs in full. While BP quarterly profits are several Billion dollars, they still consider funding the pension programs, that will give their workers what they are promised, as unimportant. British Petroleum is only an example, most major corporations do the same thing, but this is in their stockholders report. They are "allowed" to do this, by what law I do not know. This is one of those times when the Democrats hold the arms and the Republicans hold the legs of the worker, while the capitalists have their way with the funds.

All is fine and dandy for many pension funds until times get tough. Oops, the business is not doing as well as expected, then bankruptcy or more common, a merger. Pension funds are frozen so additional money can not be drained by the corporation. The problem is that the pensions are now drastically under funded, depleted by the company, often in exchange for the guarantee of continued employment for the workers, a "loan" gone bad. What money is left may then go to the Pension Benefit Guaranty Corporation.

This corporation was formed by the Federal government to pay a worker with whatever is left of a company pension funds. Corrupt company CEO's or corporate raiders usually attack the pension funds first, they are a nest of golden eggs, put there by you for your retirement. The PBGC is more often used to safeguard the corporations and their CEO's, it does little for the workers.

PBGC, was a bailout in 1974, when many companies left the taxpayer holding the bag for their unfunded pensions. Initially funded with about $30 Billion of taxpayer money, they continue today, carrying about a $16 billion deficit. Politicians say PBGC is NOT government funded. Since when can a corporation stay in business for years when they have this huge deficit? It looks like they are in the same predicament as the people they are supposed to rescue. When the PBGC finally distributes your pension, it is sometimes 50% less than you should have received, regularly 75% less, often next to nothing, a near worthless retirement. Another example of let the market rule, but only at the threat of personal decimation.

What does that problem have to do with SS? It is another example of how we are being deceived by those who want to scuttle SS, even supposedly good pension programs are in danger. Capitalists are allowed to ransack workers pension programs, laws prohibiting such practices have been passed, but don't expect results anytime soon.

Corporate retirement funding LOOPHOLES should be plugged.

CORPORATE RAIDERS

A very destructive cog in the system of retirement programs are corporate raiders. Billionaires who buy companies with the intention of dismantling them. A big target of the raider, is the pension fund and how to put those funds into their own pockets, instead of the workers that own them. As they rip the company to shreds, they suspend the pension plans and determine how they are going to shake the retirement funds loose for themselves. A typical tactic used by corporate raiders is the one previously mentioned, to declare the need for cash to continue operating, they "ask" employees if they want to continue working, so the employees "LOAN" them Billions of dollars from the retirement fund. They may continue for a while, but eventually the billions are exhausted and the company declares bankruptcy. With the pension fund depleted, the workers will now have to rethink their retirement plans. Young people have a chance, those close to retirement, are in a desperate situation. This type of activity should also be in the category of being illegal, but it is not. Certainly they have no morals when they steal the pension funds since they have no plan to help the workers, only themselves.

OUR EXTENDED LIFESPAN

Then we walk into the room with "the 800 pound gorilla"and "the nut no one is willing to crack," people living 15, 20, or 30 years longer than the SS founders ever imagined. In the 1930's, the average American lifespan was around the "retirement age", about 65 years old. The age at which a person could collect "benefits" was based on the fact that most people could not physically continue doing a days work when they reached the age of 65. All that has changed, our SS agenda must adapt if it is to be a viable program in the future.

Unfortunately, many do not earn enough to create an alternate retirement of any kind. We have to face it, for most Americans, SS is the only money they will receive when they retire. Today we have an average lifespan approaching 80 years, 15 years beyond what the system was expected to support. This great gift to society, being able to live longer, will be the DEATH of Social Security, if we do not change the retirement age.

Look at the problems we have with treating everyone fairly when it comes to the age we can retire. Today, a 20 year threshold is common with many advantaged retirement programs. Many people "retire" after 20 years and go on to find another job where they can work another 20 years and receive additional benefits. Retirement benefits for those people often fall into the category of outrageous. Two(or more) retirements plus SS. Many do it, so it must be OK. From the town employee to the Senators and Representatives of this country, many go on to other jobs that will provide a second or third source of retirement benefits, ultimately paid or subsidized by you, the taxpayer.

If a person is eligible for a retirement benefit from any government agency, anything that is taxpayer funded or subsidized, and they can receive 50% to 75% of their regular salary as retirement benefits, they should be automatically EXCLUDED from receiving any additional benefits using taxpayer funds. There is something wrong with our retirement system, and it is NOT Social Security. Workers who cannot afford retirement programs, support people that have good retirement programs, by paying taxes.

There has to be a retirement program that works for everyone, not just the select. Its true that we should not compare SS to retirement programs, but who can afford retirement programs when a worker barely makes enough to live on in 2007. All retirement programs, not just SS, must be redefined to take our extended lifespan into consideration and provide a way for ALL Americans to participate. Something sounds very wrong to me.

A few examples to review;
- A retired policeperson, 50% to over 100% of their normal pay, after 20 years.

- A retired firefighter, 50% to over 100% of their normal pay, after 20 years.
- A retired teacher, 50% to 80% of their pay.
- For Federal government workers, it varies, 50% to 80% of their pay.
- Local or state government workers, 50% to 80% of their "adjusted" pay.
- Many elected officials may have retirement benefits with as little as 6(six) years service.
- How much is your mayor provided? Do they have health benefits or cost of living attachments?
- A Senator or Representative(who usually become millionaires within a few years), have retirement and health benefits that cost taxpayers millions of dollars.

And then we proceed to Social Security. Almost all workers, who earn $40,000 to $100,000 per year, will receive about 25% of what they received while employed, from the national average of $1000 per month in 2006, to around $2000 per month for higher wage earners. Most workers have invested 6% of their pay into SS. When you add in the 6% that an employer has to pay, it is a 12% investment into SS, for your benefits. That may be a little less investment, when compared to what the advantaged workers invest, to receive a "good retirement". How much extra do the privileged people really have to invest to receive a DEFINED BENEFIT or an equivalent program, that provides 200% to 500% more than SS? It will depend on the contributions received from city, state or federal funds. That is what provides most of the difference. People that have regular jobs do not qualify for the 200% to 500% extra pay every month.

An idea.

1. Anyone who works at a full time job should receive a DEFINED benefit certificate for each year of service, without regard to his or her type of job. This certificate will contain their pay level and how much was contributed to the SS program. Their retirement compensation would be based on total earnings that have been taxed by SS and the Federal government. Total defined benefit certificates for thirty(30) years will be required to collect SS, unless there

is a medical or physical problem. We must fix the laws, before we go broke.

The present program, where the employee contributes 6% of their pay and the employer contributes a little more than that, for a total of over 12%, will be adequate to ensure a good retirement benefit, if the investments are prudent and time for the investment value to increase is 30 or 40 years. Even then, market value may severely impact the final pension value. No plan, except those guaranteed by the federal government, is without risk. Today, even those are suspect. These funds need to be removed from the Federal government general funds, they must be off limits to the politicians, they must be managed by competent people, no political hacks, insurance scam artists, or Wall Street shysters. Funds will be used to remake American jobs for our children's future.

NO POLITICS ALLOWED!

As an investment in the future of America, the funds of SS, with proper management, will provide a continuous return in the future, unlike the system we now have. Cities and states across the country borrow money from all sorts of institutions for their public works programs, why not make it the FUND for America's future, not the fund we cannot afford to support.

We are seeing a great disruption in the sphere of economics for Americans. With wages going down instead of up, corporations abandoning defined benefit retirement programs, taxes going up to support millions of federal, state and local retirement programs, most people cannot and will not be able to save enough to retire, with or without dignity. A sad state for many who work until they are 65 or 70 years old, waiting for the chance of having a few easy years of life.

There are many who say that social security is abused by people who are not qualified or have not worked long enough to collect SS. If they have worked the years required, they are entitled to the benefits. It is the process of qualification that has to be changed, so that people in need are cared for and those who abuse the system are denied. If we use the idea of a yearly certificate, all workers will

NEED 30 years paying into SS before they reach "retirement" age, not the 10 years presently required.

SOCIAL SECURITY EARNINGS LIMITS.

Another difficult problem, extending the limit that is taxed for Social Security. What is the logic behind having low wage earners pay on 100% of their income, while having high wage earners pay on 50% or less of their income? Is that what democracy does, reward the rich and tax the poor? Or is it those who make the laws are always high wage earners, you cannot expect that they won't sweeten their pie a little, or a lot. All wages should be subject to the SS tax, if you make $10,000 or $10,000,000 you should contribute your fair share, everyone pays the same percentage. Big changes are needed, real reforms to secure SS for the future.

We do have many who scam the system, in different ways. Just like you see in any large number of people, there are those who want something for nothing, and go to great lengths to get what they can steal. While they sometimes succeed, for the most part SS has proven to be an effective social program for a great number of people. We must NOT ALLOW Social Security to be scrapped, by Republicans who CARE NOTHING about the average worker.

Today more people are relying on SS as retirement income. It's future looks ominous for the next generations. Workers will not have an extra 10% or 20% to invest, required for a separate retirement program, when wages are going down and prices are going up. With living wage jobs leaving the country, and there are not many left, even fewer workers will have the ability to create a retirement fund.

Defined pension plans are history, thrown out by almost all major corporations. These retirement programs are "too expensive" for employers even though they are making billions of dollars. What took real American companies, unions of all trades and non-union workers as well, and countless labor actions, 50 years to achieve, companies abandoned at a single board meeting, with no recourse for the workers. It is not good for the bottom line.

Defined benefit programs have been demolished by the GREED of modern day capitalists. Lets level the pension system so all workers are subject to the same rules and can be rewarded in the same way, by their contribution to society. Did they work and pay into the fund for 30 or 40 years and invest their efforts into making America better, for you and me? We must be sure, above all, that Social Security remains the social safety net that it has been for 70 years.

Changing the retirement age is inevitable, it must be reflective of our longer lifespan and less physically demanding working conditions for many. All twenty year retirement programs must be changed to 30 or 40 years(except the military). We must level the playing field for all workers if any program is to remain sustainable.

To My Children;

There are many older Americans "living" on Social Security, trying to subsist on a few hundred dollars a month. They may have spent their entire life working in a job that pays minimum wage without any benefits, a common plight in our country.

Or they may have worked for one of those companies that went bankrupt, taking all the value of the pension funds with them. It was supposed to be their retirement. A lifetime of investing in their company, down the drain. We have many older people, who retired with pensions that should have been adequate, but the money is now eroded by inflation and taxes, they are struggling to survive.

If this is going to be the America that we all expected it to be, we need to stop playing favorites and have the same rules for everyone. It is not SS that is the problem, it is greed and corruption, in government, corporations and ourselves. Everyone who allows it to happen or just takes a small chunk for themselves, is guilty. Lets right the wrongs inflicted on the workers who have not worked where they have subsidized retirement programs. Keep SS strong and help improve retirement programs for ALL Americans.

Stay healthy, be happy and be kind.

Love,
Dad/Grandpa
XXXXXXXXXX X2

LETTER 7

OUR STANDARD OF *LIVING, INCREASING* OR *DECREASING*

Hi Everyone;

Well we seem to be caught in a perfect storm, the worst of many possible problems converging on everyone in America, especially those on fixed incomes. Any one of those problems by itself may be overwhelming, but we have the basic things we need to live getting too expensive for many. Things we rely on to raise our families, go to work or to do our work, costing more each day changing many peoples lifestyles.

The increases are not little, they are taking giant steps, food, healthcare, gasoline and every other item that uses oil and that includes just about everything. Some examples of the problem, the cost of a gallon of milk has increased from $3 to $4, eggs that had been a stable inexpensive food item, going from $1.00 to $2.00 a dozen, vegetables, 25 to 50% increase, even Hamburg is getting too expensive for some. Of course we have the Federal Government

107

claims of an inflation rate of TWO percent(2%), sometimes three percent. Say What? Is our government not telling the truth about inflation? They never lie, do they?

With gas over $3.00 a gallon, there are very few items that you can buy, that have not increased in price. And it is just starting to have an effect. Look out! Hold onto your pocketbooks and your wallets, but come to think of it that will be in vain, with the reality of raising prices and falling wages, there won't be anything in them to take, they will have stolen it already.

There are those who thought they were on the train GOODLIFE, having a home, a decent job, raising a family. Now the interest rates have driven them from their homes, outsourcing has taken their jobs and raising a family is so expensive we may be like Communist China, a one child rule, only ours will be because we cannot afford more than one. Raising children will be reserved for the rich and the poor, both will get help. The rich will pay for it and the poor will be provided public assistance while the middle class struggles. The train Goodlife has come to a grinding halt. It has stopped and we have not even included Iraq, gnawing away at the rails and the underpinnings of America.

Is what I see real or is the America that President Bush describes every time he makes a speech, real. NO big problems, the economy is GOOD, our financial strength is ROBUST, we are WINNING in Iraq, we have PLENTY of jobs. It really feels like I must be dreaming, I see the exact opposite, how is it where you are? PRICES, at the grocery store, at the gas pumps, every item we buy has increased, a lot,

news of more living wage jobs LOST,

DEAD US soldiers in Iraq.

Is Washington, D.C. in America?

Is the "ranch" in Crawford, Texas, in America?

This President must be living in a different America, I don't recognize his description of the conditions Americans are facing.

Politicians refuse to tell the plain facts, they are embarrassed(more likely afraid of not being re-elected) to think they have let out country get caught in a perfect storm, where their lack of leadership and failure to provide OVERSIGHT is causing extreme hardship and obstacles we cannot overcome, just like the perfect storm, there is no escape.

Our economy, our financial system(now being supported by Communist China), our imports, our medical system, and what was our industry, are out of our control. Politicians have done everything they can to prevent us from seeing the real truth, it is now upon us, our ship is sinking and we need to change course if we expect to survive as the America we know and love. They beat around the bush(no pun intended) blaming everything else, it's the fault of illegal aliens, its health care, it's unions, it's Republicans, it's Democrats, its deficit spending and on and on. The honest fact is that they have FAILED to PROTECT the American people, the very thing the Republicans say they are better at doing than the Democrats.

Our country is now MORE AT RISK than at any time during my adulthood, the last 50 years. An al Qaeda invasion of America would not come close to putting us in the precarious position that the negligent actions of our politicians have concocted. And they have the nerve to tell blatant lies to the American people saying, "Republicans will keep us safe". That is unbelievable. Democrats are just as remiss, they should have stopped the economic carnage, focused our efforts on retraining workers, and ended the senseless IRAQ WAR, long ago.

Let private industry do it, the Republican standard phrase, has given us totally unacceptable results everywhere you look. Without government oversight, that the Republicans refuse to acknowledge as essential, manufacturing, medical, financial, even educational systems have failed. The American worker is now seeing their dreams being ripped to shreds, our standard of living going down, that is every day we see prices go up, while wages go down. As the Republican politicians try to salvage what they can, to prevent their own demise, they still fail to see how they are destroying our country. Or is it they are making so much money by supporting everything that is against American workers, that is does not matter to them.

Republicans tell you they will help maintain the middleclass worker status, to ensure their living standard does not go down. They do not tell you how they will accomplish the feat, it would be a first if they did, they have never helped a worker in their lives. Democrats are rallying the union workers with the expectation that they will save the day. It's not going to happen. Without national unions they will be completely ineffective. But of course when you mention unions, every sort of black mark is conjured up by the politicians. Like we see in healthcare, we will not receive a fair shake from any corporation, without uniting as Americans, willing to help each other. Maybe we could have private enterprise "be private enterprise", not enterprise owned by a FOREIGN government, and be American.

Workers who have held manufacturing type jobs, making everything from play dough to automobiles, will have to find a different line of work. Lower wages, fewer benefits, reduced healthcare coverage, longer hours, are all being forced on our workers.

With few exceptions, manufacturing jobs as we knew them, that provided a living wage are gone forever, not until next year, or the next decade, gone forever. Heresy you say?

Sorry to say it is the absolute truth.

We have about fifty million workers in the USA that would be employed in some form of manufacturing job, that uses skilled workers. They need to make $400 per week just to be at our poverty level, with no chance of ever reaching the middle class. Then you add the cost of overhead, a normal range from 200% to 400% in the manufacturing business, plus benefits of over 30%, it would increase the cost to have you, as a worker, to over $1000 per week, but we will not even consider anything but basic wages.

Say that a factory worker in America, makes $10/hour, $400 per week. They are competing with a worker who is lucky to make $50 per week in Asia. What would you do if you owned a company and could have the same job done for 12% of the labor costs? The obvious result, to have you do the job in America, is 8 times more than the cost of a worker in an undeveloped country, without considering benefits. It is true, they have little experience, but with engineers from around the world assisting in the process, experience is quickly overcome as a make or break end result. Add in the fact that many foreign countries subsidize industries, it makes the prospects insurmountable for our manufacturing workers. There are estimates that put the cost to manufacture most goods in America, over 20 times more in a third world country.

But wait, that is only half the story. If we just consider China, forget India, Indonesia and the rest of the Pacific nations(another 2 billion people), we need to talk about the workforce. China has a population of 1.3 Billion people. There are 200 to 300 million people in the prime age for a workforce, that is as many people as we have in all age groups in America. It is obvious that we need to move away from trying to compete for manufacturing jobs that can be done in a third world country. We should take advantage of the lower costs of manufacturing, provided by others. The problem is we have given every manufacturing job and asset to a country once considered our greatest threat, the RED DAWN of Communist China. We have done it with the blessing of the Republicans, who refuse to control anything that has to do with private enterprise, and that may be a FATAL mistake, for Democracy.

Isn't it ironic, we cuddle with the communists, the biggest threat to Democracy, and bomb others who are no threat to Democracy, who are being forced into a "Bush Democracy", whether they like it or not. Stranger than fiction.

Our ports and our imports are out of control, absolutely no inspections of significance, but we are spending billions to prevent someone who may do us harm by boarding a commercial airline. Maybe that's what they were referring to when they mention that our politicians should get some "common sense". Lets put some common sense back into our government, enact voter enforced term limits, maybe a real leader will emerge. Let's concentrate on how to retrain our workers and start a national program to remake our educational system, to prepare the workers needed for the 21st century. Otherwise, we will have to accept what the capitalists and the Republicans want to provide, a lower standard of living. They will say that is nonsense, but when you look at their track record, there is no other conclusion. We are already experiencing the profound negative effects of uncontrolled capitalism and Republican politics, how do you like it?

It's not very appetizing to me.

They say history repeats itself, and in this case it is questionable if it is uncontrolled capitalism repeating itself or a totally new phenomena, much worse than capitalist abuses 100 years ago.

We should find solutions to renewable energy, providing food and drinking water for all people, making medical care available to everyone and building our own infrastructure to accommodate the next generations. Create America's living wage, one that provides our workers fair compensation and a FUTURE. At this time we in a freefall from our position as the world leaders, our morals, our economy and our technology are all declining. We have been pushed over a cliff by greedy capitalists and a government unwilling and too corrupt to help save the future for workers in America. We need people who are leaders first, not politicians first. Politicians provide tax breaks for outsourcing and they refuse to stop paying corporations to leave the country. Couple this with our own government outsourcing jobs, sometimes to foreign firms, and you quickly see that America's workers have little hope, if they stand on their own, of maintaining their standard of living. We are in trouble.

We are not providing incentives to corporations to keep good paying jobs in America. But when you think about it, they should not need incentives. They made their fortunes using this great country, they owe us, but try to collect from those billionaires, who are infected with GREEDITIS. As a result of the Bush administration actions and non-actions, our wages are going down, energy costs are going through the roof, making everything you touch much more expensive. Capitalists are using food to make ethanol, exacerbating the rising costs and creating a CATCH 22, with the consumer in the middle. The war in Iraq is putting a strain on our lives and our future, killing our young men and women, a few soldiers a week, who should be home contributing to the recovery of our economy and taking care of their families.

But NO, ABSOLUTELY NOT, the Republicans insist that they stay there until the Iraqis decide that they want to live together, not separated as they are by religious and cultural issues. We are trying to build a country, where the people are more determined to destroy themselves, than they are willing to help themselves by working together for the good of their country. Incredulous.

Iraq, a great Bush/Republican debacle, how to shoot yourself, and not in the foot.

When I look at the present WIN AT ANY COST strategy in Iraq, it reminds me of what an unscrupulous handler did to a boxer when he went into the ring. His boxer was being pummeled, his eyes closed, blood coming from his nose and mouth, but the handler had HIS goal, managing a winner, he refused to "throw in the towel" to stop the fight. When it was over, the boxer had lost his ability to fight again, the boxer suffered because of a bad decision by HIS handler. Republicans say we will be "throwing in the towel of surrender", if we withdraw from Iraq, we must "support" our troops. There is NO better way to SUPPORT OUR TROOPS, than to GET THEM OUT of harms way. Stop the killing and maiming, regardless of what OUR unscrupulous handler says, bring them home where the belong. We cannot afford to slaughter any more of our brave men and women and we cannot afford to continue spending billions of dollars that we do not have.

Does something seem wrong to you? We are borrowing billions of dollars to fight a war, and we are borrowing it from a COUNTRY that is COMMUNIST. Is there an ulterior motive as to why they are willing to help America go bankrupt? The dollar is shrinking and interest on our debt will eat future generations alive, if something else doesn't first. This war will destroy their chances of maintaining a decent standard of living, just how low it will go depends on how vigorous we pursue changing our corrupt government and how soon we STOP THE WAR.

Manufacturers should be responsible for retraining every American worker that is fired, put out of their jobs permanently, due to outsourcing. This should be considered as a cost before putting one American worker on the street. They spend a huge amount to go to China, India or elsewhere to develop workers, infrastructure and manufacturing facilities. Re-education and re-training of our workforce must be mandatory if we are to remain at a reasonable standard of living. A government imposed surcharge, to retrain each worker displaced by outsourcing, should be levied on companies who have used the resources of America to become world players.

Totally new strategies and SPECIAL SKILLS are needed to survive. The World has been transformed in the past 25 years, so significantly, that what was cutting edge is now standing still. What could only be done in the United States, can now be done in many places. Competition is with the entire world, not just our neighbors to the north and south, developing countries who are emerging with the help of the worlds industrialized nations. High on that list is the same country we are borrowing all that money from, Communist China. Imagine, the USA, borrowing money from an "emerging nation".

People we thought were leaders, should have been in a pro-active mode to retrain our workers, for the last 20 years, but with politicians fighting about who's on first, what's on second - they dropped the ball over and over, workers lose. Lets' determine what we do best, put together a collaboration of corporations that put AMERICA FIRST, to help put our workers back on track. Companies, educators, workers groups and GOVERNMENT to create the social and economic structure necessary to make our workers competitive in the future.

Stop being a country of fifty independent states, one pretending to be better than the other. We need to be America, standing as one, willing to help each other in every endeavor we undertake, if we are to maintain and improve America. Our new competition is one hundred different countries and over one half of the world's population, about 3 billion people. Just because we have always been competitive in the billion person industrialized arena, does not mean we can compete with the new manufacturing blitz, where they do not have laws that protect the workers.

A new playbook is needed. Everything that divides people to achieve a superior position has to stop, usually only a few reap the rewards of divisive societies. Those new national unions, to protect all workers, must be formed. Many problems we face are caused outside our country, national unity must prevail, or our workers and all Americans will continue to be pushed aside. We need a country united, with mastering 21st CENTURY TECHNOLOGY our goal. New ideas and products are needed to make progress. There are no short term fixes. The ultimate solution will be elevating our workers skill levels, so they can compete for jobs that are being created today. New jobs, that can become the base to keep us growing and will support our infrastructure, in dire need of improvement. Our most important and immediate goal is to be released from the ANCHOR of foreign oil.

With the money we are sending to oil producing nations and IRAQ, we could create millions of new jobs, enough to support our workers, and make them competitive again. But we need to become a "country on a mission", like when we put a man one the moon, WE made it happen. We can accomplish ENERGY INDEPENDENCE, by using American ingenuity, if we come together as Americans.

We need a renaissance in education, begin with reversing the present trend of kids dropping out of high school. If we cannot do that basic step, keep them in school,

we WILL see our standard of living decline severely. To continue having what most people enjoy today, education at every level has to change. High school kids must be shown that they will be able to better themselves if they continue with their education. Show them the future requires additional knowledge and training, beyond high school. The billions of people coming out of poverty will provide many new challenges for the working people in every country. If it is academic training or job training, it must become part of the normal transition from high school to the workforce. There seem to be few ways to impress our young people, who are the product of a "we want it all - now" society, that training and extended education is absolutely essential in this new world economy. Many adults need the same wake-up call. All workers who have been displaced, will need additional education to prosper, maybe even survive.

For our country to move forward, EDUCATION has to be FREE.

- FREE technical training,
- FREE apprentice programs,
- FREE business training programs,
- FREE college,
- American worker training for our future

Millions of American workers will be subjected to a much different lifestyle without it.

We are presently going BACKWARDS in the new world economy. Teachers and teaching administrations will have to become resilient and adaptable to our changing society, and bring a million more teachers on board. Like all of the other aspects of our society, they cannot hang onto old methods and old ideas, it is past the time for positive change.

Every student should be provided with a notebook computer, they are being manufactured by companies who are selling them for $100, so for $200, with a national order of 100 million computers, we will get a good computer. That is about the cost of a few text books that will become obsolete in a couple of years. Students will have subject information, entire sets of encyclopedias, reference books on all subjects, and the latest techniques of assimilating information, sitting on their desks, a few clicks away.

Students should be able to progress at their own rate, not the rate of 30 students from all backgrounds and nationalities. Teachers will need to allow maximum flexibility for their teaching assignments, many of the teachers union rules need to be deleted or updated. State colleges or colleges that are assisted with public funds have to be free to those who are willing to devote their time and energy to obtain good grades. Training in a specific new technology or a two year trade apprentice program, will be mandatory and free, for all who graduate from high school. Aid to the firms that hire and train these graduates, will have to be provided. Options of serving in the military or serving society for two years after completing high school should be available. These things are not new, what would be new is that all our young people would have an obligation and an opportunity to continue being involved in some positive way, with active roles in our communities, not just the select few. It would also be new and American, for us to provide EQUAL OPPORTUNITIES to all people.

During the 1950's/60's, we were shocked by Japan and it's ability to excel with manufacturing expertise. Twenty years later they were producing some of the best products in the world. Great products, with the aid of American ingenuity, and at competitive prices, even though they had to import ALL their raw materials. That was one of our first large off-shore outsourcing jobs of American technology. There were cries that the Japanese were taking over America, we needed to stop helping our competitors. Many manufacturing jobs were lost and the auto industry has never recovered, but it was not the economic disaster many had suggested. That kind of competition is good, two countries with similar standards of living, trying to make better products for the world. That rise of Japanese manufacturing does not "hold a candle" to the new world CRISIS. Now we are faced with slave labor in manufacturing, not countries that have to maintain reasonable worker wage and safety standards.

Our present politicians have had their chance to lead. They have proven that they are unable to perform, unable to comprehend, unable to work together, like children who take "their ball" and go home if they cannot have it "their way." Leaders are needed who understand the new world economy, its challenges and its opportunities. We must return to the American ideals that made us a great country and the UNITED STATES OF AMERICA.

Outsourcing is the LOWERING of American worker wages and calling it something else. Private companies who provide the same service at less cost, are doing it by paying their help less, they work longer without overtime pay or they do not receive benefits, like healthcare. When a person is being displaced by outsourcing is it because they have invented a better way to make the product or make the person doing the job more efficient? No, someone is going to do it for less. Yet we do not seem to think that anything is wrong. We object loudly when they say they are going to reduce a workers pay, but outsourcing his job is OK. Say what? Every job in our government is being "outsourced", except the ones that should be, the politicians and their political appointees. Republicans were unsuccessful at "privatizing", so they will do it by calling it something else and give all jobs to private companies, even to foreign companies that may not be private. From the local city governments to our federal government, outsourcing is destroying all American workers ability to earn a living wage. They claim it's budget constraints, that is another word for the inability to plan.

Local governments think they are doing great when they have something done for less, but it is usually at some workers expense that they made it happen. If a job is going to a firm that does not pay a fair wage and provide reasonable benefits, then they should not be considered as an alternate source to do the work. Many government agencies and small city departments outsource without any consideration as to who will do the work. As a result, many workers lose their jobs that go to underpaid or less qualified workers.

That is a practice we should not allow, to satisfy "budget" or other monetary constraints. Put the politicians and their political appointees considering this type of activity out of office, they are un-American.

There is another "outsourcing gimmick" that is being explored by many state governments. They are leasing our highways, that have been built with public funds, to foreign entities, government or other. They are trying to make up shortfalls in their budgets caused by poor management, by elected officials or the people who control the states. This should be declared unconstitutional - at all levels of government. Public assets must remain public, no matter who the politician is that is trying to rip off the public, because of their callous behavior. Our SECURITY and protecting our assets from foreign control is far more important than providing an escape mechanism for incompetent politicians.

There was a joke some time ago, that went something like this: This person was very gullible and would buy things of questionable value, when they bought something we would often say "the next thing they are going to sell you is the Brooklyn bridge".

Well that does not seem to be so funny anymore, we now have to watch every move these politicians make, or some terrorist may end up collecting the tolls, or shutting it down when they please. And that's no joke.

To My Children;

All children will face many obstacles in this exciting but dangerous 21st century. If we are going to prosper as a nation, cultural, political and religious walls will have to come down, in the same way the walls between nations have been removed. By working together as one nation, with dedication to a better world, we can become a world leader again. If we do not work together, our lifestyles will be significantly changed, the infamous two class system, rich and poor, will emerge. We cannot let that happen.

The American Dream was not a dream, it was a reality for the millions of workers who experienced it in the 20th century. It must be reinvigorated for the 21st century, and our young people can do it.

Be happy, stay healthy and be kind,

Love,
Dad/Grandpa
XXXXXXXXXX X2

LETTER 8

TERM LIMITS OR CORRUPTION

Hi Everyone;

One thing we have not heard this election cycle is any talk about TERM LIMITS. It was very popular so time ago, but there is nothing at all mentioned now. Why, you ask? Well, they will not fire themselves, or promise to do so if no one demands term limits and insists they pass a law to make it happen. We need term limits, for all elected officials. There is a great saying that fits Washington politics, "Absolute power will absolutely corrupt." Someone's quote, I do not know who, but they must have been familiar with our political system. And by the way, I may have mentioned that quote before, it seems to apply to a lot of subjects in Washington.

Incumbents become very accustomed to the power and privilege that goes with the positions of elected officials, especially a senator or a representative. There are not many places in the world that an elected official, has the power of our congressional members. When you add in the very important SENIORITY ranking, they become kings with their own servants. Incumbents have a lot to gain over a "freshman" coming into office. They rule the roost, they become committee chairpersons who will decide which bill will produce the most votes during the next election, what legislation is essential, will it be sent to a hearing to delay passage(the oppositions bill), when should it go to the floor for debate or will it be scuttled. Partisanship rules supreme.

It is very important how long they have held their office. The amount of money they can raise for campaigning is directly dependant on what committees they are on and how much influence they will have at getting the "right vote" for the lobby. A politicians RE-ELECTION campaign starts the day they take office. Money needs to start flowing immediately. Higher ranking on significant committees, will mean more money from the lobbyists and special interests, who have something to gain or lose from the law or rule being considered.

At this time our congress is out of control, there is not a semblance of honesty, not a single public official who can or does tell the truth. Time and again we see our public officials caught in one scandal after another, a Democrat hiding $100,000.00 of bribe money, in a freezer in his home, to a Republican providing influence for government contracts worth millions of dollars. What do they receive as punishment, usually a slap on the hand and an admonition, "you better not do it again, until after the next election".

It has now come to light, stated by presidential candidates, that briefings prepared for the start of the Iraq invasion were not even read by many in congress, who then voted on this enormously tragic action. The life and death of our soldiers was NOT important enough for them to take the time to become fully informed so they could make a sound decision, on a bill to go to WAR. How many wish they had done the job that we sent them to Washington to do? If they had done their job properly, they would not have the blood of thousands of dead and wounded American soldiers on their hands. When you add in the destruction of Iraqi civilians and their homes, would they have made a different decision if they had been diligent and did their jobs? All reasonable people say IRAQ was a blunder of enormous proportions, thank you senator. That is business as usual in Washington, a good example of why we should have term limits, it shows how incumbents become complacent and irresponsible. What a way to run a country.

Who is doing the peoples business that should transpire in congress every day? Are the elected officials who spend months in their districts campaigning, doing the work? Or is it the Senator who flies into Washington, for the day, to vote on critical legislation that he has not even read? During the presidential campaigns we have 25% of our senators out campaigning for months. By the time the presidential election takes place, some senators will have been campaigning for two(2) years. And that is not a few hours here and there, it is full time, plus. If they can be away from their jobs for months at a time, do we need their services at all? Maybe that would benefit the country more than anything, send them all home, permanently. WRITE a piece of legislation? DEBATE an important bill being considered? READ the bill? If I am going to cast a deciding vote, do I have to read it first? VOTE? Sorry, I am out of town, but "I will see what my staff can do. We will try to fit it in."

We even have Senators who are absent for weeks and months because of illness. Certainly we should have sick time, but if you are unable to work for extended periods of time in the private sector, you will be replaced by someone else until you return. Shouldn't someone be assigned, by law, to that position until he or she recovers and can realistically comprehend what they are voting on? The replacement should be there until the next election, when term limits would fix the problem.

Who REALLY writes the bills in congress? In the case of the prescription drug law for Medicare the pharmaceutical companies wrote the bill, while the President refused to let any of our Democratic representatives participate. When they were done, it was a take it or leave it decision given to our legislators, our so called "lawmakers".

Our energy policy was written by Bush and Chaney oil buddies, by the looks of things they did a good job, for the oil industry. Our President has been saying we need an energy policy that will make us independent of foreign oil. The policies we have today are going to make us independent alright, if oil continues its upward spiral we will be walking to work, we won't be able to afford gas. I wonder if that would satisfy this Presidents goals.

How can our legislators make rational decisions about a bill that is a 1000 pages of legalize and contains amendments that add hundreds or thousands of pages more? They debate the bill for days or weeks, adding one amendment after another. The amendments are usually to counteract provisions of the main bill or aimed at making the bill meaningless. They never even read the first 1000 pages, so how can they assimilate 1000's of pages more? Then in the final hours when they are ready to vote on the issue, someone adds another 1000 page amendment. Without time to study the amendment they vote and approve items that are totally unrelated or the bill no longer reflects the original desire of the legislation. It happens a lot more than anyone would want to believe.

Who finances the "investigative jaunts" for congress and their staff? Who provides the millions of dollars for media ads, designed so you will put pressure on your congressperson, to support or defeat bills being submitted? Who provides the most campaign money for the representative or senator, writing the legislation, or inserting an amendment into a bill that a group or business needs enacted? It may be done in the dead of night, illegally, an amendment is added. The pressure cookers of congress, the Washington LOBBYISTS. It is difficult for a congress person, to write a bill that is for America, when you have people from many different special interest groups, who exert constant pressure to influence the outcome. In some cases, those applying the pressure and providing the perks to the congressperson may not even be citizens of this country. It seems that there is no end to the amount of money or special favors that can be handed out to our senators and representatives for "a favorable vote". In the end, the language of the bill is not for the good of the people. Some business or industry has gained another "loophole" for their owners, CEO's or stockholders.

The lobbyists are high paid lawyers, retained by any and all significant groups or business in America, from the Boy Scouts to Microsoft. They live in the congress person's pockets. They are there every day, at any time, for any reason, they apply any means they can, often illegal, to help pass or defeat a bill. Do you think your email or letter, has the same persuasion as this high priced lawyer who works for a lobby, has money by the suitcase, wines, dines, and cajoles the person who is supposed to represent the American people? Not a chance.

We need to start the process of putting term limits in place at the next election. Everyone, your friends and your neighbors, must be registered to vote. There will not be a new American Party in time for the next election, so it does not matter, if you want to be a Republican, that is your choice, likewise for Democrats or Independents. To enact term limits all politicians need to be treated the same. Please, do not listen to any of them, no more rhetoric, the time of promises is over, done, finished. Politicians have promised for decades to enact term limits, they have broken every promise, we will send them into the land of "no returns".

Incumbent politicians, like many other leaders, have led the working people of America down a road to certain ECONOMIC RUIN, by allowing corporations to decimate their wage structure, reduce healthcare coverage and put their pension plans in shambles. American companies must have some obligation to their workers, as well as to their stockholders, it should be a law.

Our present day elected officials have failed us miserably. Or is it simply that there is nothing they can do, there are no American companies left in our country.

We cannot and should not feel obligated to any incumbent. Kick them out, a fresh start is needed. All young people must get going, start a petition:

We will not vote for any incumbent, not a Democrat, Republican or Independent. You are fighting for YOUR future. Politicians refuse to pass term limits, and they are too powerful for any individual citizen to challenge, much less defeat. With enough people agreeing to hold the line and not vote for any incumbent, we will have voter enforced term limits!

Starting with the next time you enter the voting booth, do NOT vote for any incumbent, not one. It does not matter if they are your mother, brother, or your only source of income. No second term or tenth term, until we have regained control of our government. If we start an online effort today, and we do not re-elect any politician at the National level, we will remove one half of all incumbent representatives and one third of all senators, in just one election cycle. Everyone has to maintain that process for at least 6 years, the re-election period of senators, only then will we have a clean slate. We have to be steadfast in our resolve to change our system that has been corrupted. Hold the line,

Do not return any incumbent to any congressional seat. If we do this simple process, we will not have a single re-elected official, improperly influencing our government with seniority. While experience is very important, congress has proven time and again, that seniority in Washington, is a disaster for America. From our state to the national level, anyone who may use seniority to influence our laws, as well as those that are partnering with the lobbyists of industry to change our laws beyond recognition, for special interests, will be removed.

This effects the President, he or she will not have the party regulars, Republican, Democrat, or other, to do their bidding. We may have a chance at American people first laws. It is like your computer, when you have a virus or a worm in your system, you may have to re-install the operating system. Sometimes some of your most important information will be lost. But if you want a good working system, it may be necessary.

Are you ready?

"But we will lose out, our senator has years of seniority, he brings a lot of money to our district, they are wonderful persons." Those are the phrases that demonstrate why we are seeing the decline of America, "if it does not benefit me, it is not good". A major problem in America today, those words suggest how we act. Everything we want is based on the ME attitude. Someday it has to go back to the WE thought process, good for everyone, if we are to survive as THE UNITED STATES OF AMERICA. It is time for America to go back to the times when "the American way" meant something, something good, not evil. Like passing laws that benefited everyone, including, the environment, our children, the future of America. We need to come together, elect new leaders and pass laws that will put America on the path to prosperity again. We need to be competitive in the new world of commerce, that is a major challenge in the 21st century.

We cannot do it if our leaders have an agenda that is exclusively for themselves.

OUR AGING LEADERS.

We have people in congress who have been there for a very long time, they have been re-elected many times by their constituents. Being elected to a second term, is much easier than it is to be successful the first time, records show that incumbents are re-elected by a large margin. As a result, we have many senators who have been there so long they become chronologically "old" in their position. When we have critical thinking functions that need to be accomplished, like piloting an aircraft, we look for someone with quick thinking and understanding to make it happen. They do not allow pilots to fly a commercial aircraft after they reach age sixty(60), the safety of hundreds of lives is in their hands. Wouldn't it make sense to have a similar rule when MILLIONS of lives are on the line, not "just" a few hundred, it's our lives and millions of other Americans!

Shouldn't politicians retire just like most Americans at age 65? We should impose an upper age limit of sixty-five, for anyone running for Senator, Representative or President. Trying to administer a country of 300 million citizens, has proven to be a challenge for those who have achieved being elected President of the United States. It is certainly stressful and requires that conflicting information be evaluated and acted on, where the future is on the line, for our country and all children. That is not a place for those who are on the decline of their lives. And make no mistake about it, by the time you have reached age sixty-five, everyone is on a downward slope. Can you find any honest person, over the age of 65 who will say their abilities, in just about anything, certainly physical, are not going down? While mental abilities are more important, your though process does not function as well when you age, especially when you have problems, like those that cause physical pain.

Anyone who is over 65 years old, can not be sworn into any public office, at least at the national level. That would allow the president of our country to be as old as 69, if we enact term limits, 73 if we do not. We would still have some politicians in office after they are 70, but to have a seventy five(75) or eighty(80) year old senator, representative or president making decisions, even though they have obvious deficits, on critical issues with our nations future at stake, is ludicrous. There may be some rare occasion when a person over 65 is still "in their adult greatness", but it is very evident that we decline in many ways as we age, and we are at a much greater risk of developing a debilitating illness. Should we risk our lives, our nation and our children's future, to continue with politics as usual? We have had too many bad examples of this problem in our government to let it continue. I would call it "committing an American tragedy," if we do not enforce age limits on all politicians, with the President's office heading the list.

Every incumbent politician who wants to "continue to serve their country by being in politics" can act as advisors to the people that take their place. Make it part of the process, it would be very beneficial for America, people who are dedicated to putting America back on track are desperately needed.

LEGISLATION

While we are limiting things, we need to limit the physical size of all legislation, every bill that may become law cannot contain more than 100 pages. What? That's impossible you say. In addition, it has to be written in plain English, so ordinary people who are being affected by the law, can understand it. "But what will we do with all those elaborate phrases and sentences that say one thing but mean another, that we learned in law school and so skillfully honed as a politician?" Put them where they belong, in the rubbish bin. If the issue being considered cannot be defined in 100 pages, without LEGALIZE, give it to some grade school students, they will fix it. Today it is common for a bill to contain 1000's of pages. Someone, somewhere, must be trying to hide something very bad if it takes 1000 pages to disguise the real effect the bill will have if it is passed. Then to add to the hodge podge are many infamous amendments that railroad our legislative process. That process has become so cumbersome and corrupt, that most people in Washington do not know what the real effect a piece of legislation will have. There are so many pages, even illegal additions, placed there in the middle of the night, so many amendments, it takes weeks or months after they pass the bill for them to realize what they have done. Or some loophole raises it's ugly head and shows unexpected and disastrous results, for the taxpayers.

Let's get back to basics, pass laws that will be for the good of all Americans, written so everyone will understand what the rules are, not laws that have to be interpreted by lawyers and one judge after another, then reversed by the "Supreme Court".   Why should you need a doctorates degree in law, a lawyer, to interpret or explain our laws? Of course that's why they write them like they do, it keeps the lawyers in business, and good ordinary people out of politics and in the dark.

- We must enact laws that limit all public office holders to two(2) terms in office. It is already a law for the Presidents office, we will not be breaking new ground, just firming up what we have.
- Ban all groups or persons from our nations capital that are formed to lobby elected or appointed officials. BAN lobbyists.
- For senators, representatives and the president, write a law that sets the upper age for anyone taking the oath of office, at the national level, to sixty five(65) years old.
- Limit the physical size of a bill in our congress to 100 pages before it can be considered for debate or vote. An amendment should follow the same rule.

Write all laws in plain English, not legalize, so everyone has a chance to read and understand the effects it will have on their lives. The English language can be very effective, even using words that most people understand or you can look up in an ordinary dictionary.

To my children;

We all have our favorite politician who is a true American, working for the good of all our people. It will be unfortunate to lose their seniority when important programs that are for the people are being promoted. From education to pensions and everything in between, many long term politicians have worked very hard to pass laws favorable to all Americans. Some will be out of office for the first time in years. They should become part time advisors, it would not change their work schedules very much. We may find some true patriots if we open the doors to congress. All children are being shortchanged by our GREED and careless disregard of what their future will be. There is no time for further debate, get involved today, do not cast a vote for any incumbent. Start the movement for voter enforced term limits, today.

Stay healthy, be kind and be happy,

Love,
Dad/Grandpa
XXXXXXXXXX X2

LETTER 9

ENERGY - OIL, NUCLEAR OR SUSTAINABLE

Hi everyone;

When its time for heating season in some parts of the country, your energy bills, your energy consumption, will go up and those in the south will go down. Someone, somewhere is making maximum use of America's energy resources, year round. We need to take a serious look at how to improve our energy supply and what energy will be available for our children and their children. "America   is very much like me, getting old and running on empty." We have had 100 different alternatives for energy, but they do not work because they are not "cost effective". What does cost effective mean? Is it like every other current capitalist endeavor, if we cannot make a huge profit, we will not do it? It is time to get over it and solve our energy problem now, not next year, now.

We need extensive energy programs, drilling for oil, for geothermal power and natural gas, make coal a gas or liquid that can run cars and trucks or supply clean burning energy for our power plants. NUCLEAR power plant construction should start today. Nuclear power works, its environmentally clean, we have the technology, lets make it happen. They can be decommissioned, if necessary, when we develop a real alternative to oil. Oil will not be easy to replace, it is a fantastic natural resource.

Drilling for more oil, in many of those places deemed off limits because of environmental concerns, should start today, by Executive Order, clearly stating the menacing energy crisis that besets our country. We must not proceed in a haphazard way, but we must consider that America's future is in balance. Of course all the oil in the world will not help if we do not have the capacity to refine it, so construction of refineries must also begin today. Developing nations "throw all caution to the wind" to get energy for their countries, we cannot watch them destroy our economy and the environment, while we sit and allow our country to be destroyed by costly energy. The most immediate benefit from the executive order, even before drilling starts, will be the decrease in the cost of oil due to speculation, it could be significant.

We have many sun, wind and water possibilities that should be in use today, but without national planning, not much will happen. Political and economic games of our politicians and private industry looking for quick dollars, will not work. We need

Everyone working together to solve our energy crisis. We have already had massive brownouts from normal home and industry electrical consumption. And now, without any thought, whatsoever, we are introducing vehicles that are more "efficient" because they use electric power to supplement gasoline. It may be good as long as it does not, repeat DOES NOT, involve using electricity from our existing power grids. They are already at the breaking point. Do we think we can convert our millions of cars to electric without massive changes to our electric power generation output? Think again.

One half of our electricity presently comes from coal. Will we be swapping one bad choice, foreign oil, for another bad choice, dirty coal(using our present coal burning standard) to increase electric output using coal to run those electric cars? China is polluting their country, and much of the world, by burning coal in an irresponsible manner. Are we going to join in on the decimation of the world's environment?

Nuclear is the most effective proven solution. The problem of nuclear waste and the perception that nuclear power plants are not safe need to be solved. Fifty(50) years of nuclear power generation, around the world, has proven them to be safe. Accidents involving nuclear power plants, have been from human mistakes, not the generation system. A program, on a global scale with all nations that use nuclear energy, to solve the nuclear waste problem, needs to be started today, deactivation of nuclear waste is imperative. It must be an International Priority.

A solution to the nuclear waste problem should be resolved while we build our NEXT 200 NUCLEAR POWER PLANTS, nuclear power generation should be used for water desalination and/ or purification as well as generating electricity, they will provide electricity and water, both desperately needed in many parts of our country. It is not new, desalination and purification are obtained from nuclear power plants in operation today.

With 300 nuclear power plants in operation, yes we have about 100 NUCLEAR POWER PLANTS in operation now in America, we would have a good start to becoming independent from imported oil for electricity. By shifting the energy source from oil to nuclear, we can use domestic oil for transportation. If we then increase our ability to obtain more electricity from coal by making it environmentally clean, we cane ensure we have enough to power all those electric cars. We could be INDEPENDENT FROM FOREIGN OIL, within 20 years. Coal currently supplies one half of the energy we use for electricity. Only then will we be able to power America so we can move forward. Before that happens, an alternate renewable energy source to power our autos should emerge.

TV commercials that show a salesman plugging their autos into a household outlet to be recharged, are nonsense. It will work for the first cars off the assembly line, but the power system will fail, national brownouts and blackouts will follow, with any sizable number of cars recharging their batteries. Powering totally electric autos using our existing power generation network is completely irrational, it will not work. If we do not start building nuclear plants NOW we have to answer these questions;

1. Who will build America's power plants, desperately needed today?
2. What energy source will be used?
3. When will they be ready to power the new electric cars and fill our insatiable quest for more energy?

We must get a lot smarter than we have been for the last 50 years, to provide enough electrical energy to power 100's of millions of cars. We have not scratched the surface of developing a REAL alternative to oil. "So, not to worry, we have another idea on how to solve our gasoline problem, ethanol! Some hybrids can run on anything, including cooking oil, our problem is solved." What a brilliant idea. We are spending billions of dollars, developing energy that is produced with food. We convert edible products into ethanol so we can run our 10 mile per gallon SUV's, forcing the cost of food to go out of sight. Those amber waves of grain, to be used for ethanol, will have to stretch from ocean to ocean, and into the ocean, to make an impact on our oil imports while sustaining our grain consumption and exports.

Ethanol will not make a proverbial "drop in the bucket" in our effort towards solving the imported oil crisis. This may be a great feel good solution, but it is no substitute for importing trillions of gallons of gas per year. Without emergency measures, by a President with an AMERICA FIRST conviction, who will forget the Arab interests(they have forgotten us), the future for the American energy supply looks dismal.

We are devoting precious development time and dollars, to build plants to produce ethanol, from corn, an effort that will reduce our oil imports by an unknown amount. Why is it unknown? Estimates of net fuel obtained when producing ethanol from corn, depends on how much energy it took to cultivate, harvest, and process the crop into ethanol. Realistic estimates of NET energy gain are very low, about 10% is a high number used. Using rough estimates, that means it takes 9 gallons of fuel, imported or other, to produce 10 gallons of fuel, for a net gain of 1 gallon. That may be OK if it does not affect our food supply, but some estimates even show there is a net energy LOSS when converting corn to ethanol. If we concentrate on making ETHANOL from waste or vegetation that grows naturally, without significant cultivation, that would be a major step forward. Otherwise, using FOOD for ethanol, FORGET IT! It is another capitalist charade.

Everyone looks at Brazil and says if they can do it, why can't we? Brazil makes their energy from sugar cane, that is far more effective than corn when its being used to produce ethanol, 6 to 8 times more efficient. We would have to replace every crop of our southern states to grow sugar cane in the quantity needed to make a dent in imported oil.

Sugar fields in Florida are considered as a significant source of water pollution, involving the entire southern part of Florida, the Everglades, with contamination flowing into the Gulf of Mexico. Presently, the federal and state governments are spending billions to clean up the sugar companies mistakes and complete disregard for the environment. It would be a bad solution, trying to fix a bad problem.

CONSERVATION.

We cannot forget the most immediate reduction in oil imports will come from conservation. As one of the most wasteful societies on the planet, it is time to step up and take all the energy saving steps we can today, it is up to each individual to make it happen. There are 100's of things we can do today to save energy, they just need action.

First will be our personal habits, change the attitude "if you are done with it, throw it away". If it can be used by someone else, make it available to them. Use fewer paper and plastic items that we throw out after one use, take shorter showers with cooler water, use "green" reusable bags when shopping, walk or ride a bicycle when possible, eat less - its good for you and the country, we waste enough food to feed a small nation. Get serious about recycling, it can save a lot of energy. Some simple steps you can do that will make an immediate difference. Here are just a few for the home; Lower the thermostat a couple of degrees for those who heat, raise it for those who cool, install programmable thermostats, keep heating and cooling systems clean with regular filter changes and check-ups, install additional insulation and more energy efficient windows - the most significant area of energy loss in cold(and hot) climates, use energy efficient appliances and lights. The internet has hundreds of other practical things to do.

A simple cost effective, energy efficient tankless hot water heater for use at every hot water faucet would save energy and water, it should be developed and made available. Make it part of a national BUILDING CODE, that is now essential to make the most of our energy and natural resources. Every new building should be energy efficient and built from renewable materials, regardless of what area of the country is involved.

Conserving at every level is necessary and we do not have to make great leaps forward, steady consistent growth towards total energy and economic independence, but it must start today. Over sixty percent of our imported oil goes to transportation. Increasing the café standard 10 miles per gallon, today, would make a significant improvement. Auto manufacturers will say it cannot be done without major disruptions, but it MUST be done. Autos only make up part of the fuel use, with trucks, trains and airplanes consuming the remainder.

Many airlines are using planes that are 30 years old, where the engines efficiency does not compare to what is available today. These older engines should be sent into mothballs. And while we are putting things into mothballs, we should have a national program that scraps all automobiles that do not get 15 miles per gallon of gas and outlaw new ones that do not meet that standard.

We have to rethink the way we move people and products. Results of deregulation of the airline industry has led to a calamity in the airports, a catastrophe for the public. They have cut flights to make certain every plane will carry its full capacity of passengers, maximizing profit at customer expense. On time arrival, passenger convenience and SAFETY are no longer of any importance. With any minor disruption in the system, like heavy rain at a major airline hub, thousands of travelers are delayed, become stranded or are severely inconvenienced. All for the goal of more profit.

Railroads were mostly abandoned many years ago, but they are the most energy efficient means of transportation we have. If we provide the same subsidies and incentives to the railroad industry as we did airlines, they could put economical rail transportation back on the map. Railroads need to be revitalized and rejuvenated to provide an energy efficient transportation system, a needed national option to air.

Another alternative to consider for development, a new national highway program, that incorporates the latest technologies for moving people and goods. A trucktrain without rails, using dedicated lanes of the interstate highways for new tractors and trailers linked together without the restrictions of length. With computer controlled tractors, that can be coupled together when needed, GPS guidance systems and crash avoidance technology available today, trucktrains to transport cargo, that may include you, in your car, will provide an alternative mode of transportation. They will be able to use the same interstate routes as the traveling public, but separated by physical road barriers. It could open a totally new approach to the efficiencies produced by the rail system, but without the rails.

Many simple solutions are needed for our roads, like eliminating toll booths that back up traffic for miles, pouring gas down the drain. Manual tolls on highways, bridges, tunnels, anything that causes delays on the road, should be eliminated. Using transponders is very effective and eliminates backups. The capability to recognize your vehicle should be mandatory, in every state and across the nation. An electronic VIN, connected with automatic billing as part of a national highway system, would solve the problem. Not a big deal. Work together, no individual states,

THE UNITED STATES.

High occupancy lanes on highways are used in most congested roads going into our cities, in all parts of the country. We need to have a directive to make it mandatory, that all automobiles being used for daily commutes into and out of the city at peak traffic times, be HOV, with a minimum of three(3) people. Use the internet, with UPS or FEDEX for some organizational help to make it happen, it could be accomplished in weeks. We had 55 MPH speed limits during the last big oil crisis, which was nothing compared with today, should we use it again? Those are some simple examples, you will have many more.

We have seen signs that something is wrong, in our country and around the world, for decades.

- Smog, chocking the people of major cities.
- Cancer causing hazardous and industrial waste sites, everywhere.
- Polluted rivers, lakes and streams.
- Oil spills, creating environmental disasters.
- Our drinking water becoming contaminated by chemicals in the gasoline. An environmental hazard, MANDATED by law. It sounds unreasonable, is it?
- Power plants pouring acid rain over neighboring communities and countries. A lot has been cleaned with better technology, make it "totally clean", we would then have centuries of energy for electricity, for America, using clean coal technology. A government led program should be started to make it happen, even if it does not make the "oil boys" happy.
- New power plants and drilling for oil are restricted, environmental concerns. Just having a program that evaluates off-shore drilling will bring some of the speculation that causes price increases overnight, to subside. The echo friendly wind farm off the coast of Massachusetts, rejected because the towers, placed offshore, will spoil the pristine scenery, is an example of nonsense that has to stop, they will not be able to see through the smog, much less see the scenery. It is time to rethink all alternatives, the time for procrastination is over, we must take positive actions that produce positive results,

IMPORTING OIL TO BURN, MUST STOP.

Where is the leadership in our country? Can they see their hand in front of their face? Are they too busy fighting each other, trying to preserve their jobs, while America struggles with its energy woes? Our country is going to live or die on their decisions regarding energy. This administration is riddled with people who cannot make decisions that are for the good of our country, throw them out, lock, stock and barrel. Common sense, long ago discarded by politicians, must prevail.

To satisfy the worlds demand of energy, we need solutions, big and small, and people willing to take the extra effort to make them happen. China, India and Indonesia may be the source of our present economic problems, but as we are reminded every day, they also represent the opportunity for American companies to create new markets, and they can capture them without leaving America. ECONOMIES run on ENERGY and without an adequate source, no country can prosper and help their citizens elevate to a higher standard of living. Companies have gone to these third world countries for the unlimited supply of cheap labor and the potential market of billions of people coming out of poverty. Capitalists, or the governments that provide companies with slave labor, do not care where the energy is coming from to power this massive explosion of manufacturing, as long as they are making profits. It is already an environmental nightmare.

While most corporations have chosen to desert this country, we should look to promising technologies and with the help of government initiatives, yes, reverse the idea that only private enterprise can make it happen, form groups of companies, to become technological leaders-again, especially in sustainable energy. These companies will be aided with federal funding, to ensure that the technology developed remains in this country, not stolen, as companies are presently doing with all our technology.

The corporate/government partnership works very well when properly controlled, if no one is allowed to make and break the rules and laws as they see fit. Many nations have put that idea to work and are now leaders in several advanced fields, producing great products that dominate in world technology and production. The key to success is always the training and education of the workforce.

WATERPOWER

There are many rivers in our country and most of them could be used for power generation, very few are. We do not have to build giant dams, small diversions of water in strategic places will allow power generation to service small communities. If we go back to the start of the industrial revolution in the United States, the energy used to power the great Mile of Mills, in Lowell, Massachusetts, was water. Directly powering 1000's of machines producing textiles; carding and combing, spinning, looms for weaving, dyeing, the entire mill, over a mile long, running on water. Countless other factories in New England were powered by this same river, the Merrimack.

Although this river provided a great energy resource to the capitalists who built and ran the textile factories, they destroyed the river by indiscriminate dumping of their industrial waste into the river, contaminating the water with all sorts of debris, including caustic cleaners and dyes. I can remember seeing the river turn an eerie green or a bright yellow on many occasions. The river became severely polluted, killing the fish and rendering the water unfit for humans, or for any life. Dams prevented the salmon from going up the river to spawn, but water quality would have destroyed the fish even if they could negotiate the dams, so it was a double dose of death for these salmon. No one knows what the influence of this pollution was or is on human health.

Many poisons continue to flow into the sea where countless fish are exposed to these accumulating toxins. Billions of fish are caught and eaten, by people of every country around the world. How long can the oceans, and all people, survive these biological attacks? The signs of our degrading environment show up in the fish we harvest, with the chemicals of our industrial waste found in their bodies. Capitalists did what they always do, destroy human and natural resources, FOR PROFIT. The potential energy available from all rivers is enormous, waiting for someone to re-harness the power, instead of just having it flow to the sea. Will it or can it be cost effective?

Everything that has the potential of reducing our dependence on oil, that decreases the burning of fossil fuel, and is above all, SUSTAINABLE, needs to be evaluated.

Some of you may remember the lumber yard we had in our area. While it was relatively small, they processed the lumber from logs into finished wood, for several communities and their home builders. This entire process, from the large saws for the logs, to the finishing planes, was powered by a small 2 acre pond. The power of flowing water, including the tides of our oceans and the power of the sun, has tremendous energy. How to harness them efficiently should be done on a national scale, with help to the most promising solutions, and not after years of study, today. We need to become energy independent, some help is already here, America can do it, lets show the way for the rest of the world.

Our next president cannot be tied to the oil companies and foreign oil. He or she must have the health and well being of all people at heart and they should have a clear vision of how to approach the myriad of problems we face. We will not solve them overnight, it is going to take a long time to get out of George Bush's quagmire. America and our lifestyle are in jeopardy. We need to resume our world leadership in the 21st century, but it cannot be done with our present government, that condones corporate corruption. That's why we need everyone to step up and join the effort, not only for energy independence for America, but for independence from CORPORATE GREED, that is destroying our living wage jobs, and our future.

Your vote is important, your choice as to who can best lead our country, is crucial. Challenges for all workers are many, and they cannot be met without everyone's help. A plan on how to solve our energy crisis is more important than any other, after we leave Iraq.

To my children;

We have seen corporations remove all our living wage jobs. To add insult to injury, the cost of oil has broken the budgets of everyone who has to work for a living. Gasoline was 12 to 15 cents a gallon when I drove my first car. A far cry from today by any measure, who knows what it will be tomorrow. Over the years, attempts have been made to create competitive electric cars, solar heating for homes, and many alternate energy sources. Most have been discarded because they were not "cost competitive or cost effective."

We are now in a situation where we MUST stop burning imported oil and ALL FOSSIL FUEL. Energy costs are adversely affecting our world standing and our standard of living.

Our hard earned dollars continue to decline in value with every barrel of oil and every cargo container we import. When you throw in global warming, it is no longer a choice, our future is at stake. In fact, the world's future is at stake if everyone does not stop burning fossil fuel.

Stay healthy, be happy and be kind,

Love,
Dad/Grandpa
XXXXXXXXXX X2

LETTER 10

REPUBLICAN OR
UNION MAN

Hi Everyone;

In a discussion with my staunch Republican neighbor, who worked for 30 years in management for one of America's foremost companies, proclaimed he was a union man and had his union card to prove it. My first comment to him was, "either you do not really understand what it is to be a Republican or you are a wolf in sheep's clothing, pretending to be a union worker, while doing the bidding of management." It is an oxymoron to say you are "A REPUBLICAN UNION MAN." Of course there are millions who will disagree, and yes, there may be legitimate Republican union workers who still believe in the tooth fairy and that being a Republican is the way to stand on your own two feet.

The real problem is that these workers fail to see, nothing the Republican party programs stand for, has any positive effect on the working person. Like cutting taxes for the rich, so they can create jobs, it is a bigger joke than waiting for the Easter bunny to bring you some Easter eggs. Nor do a majority of today's young workers know that most of the advances in wages and benefits for working people came about because of the Democratic Party, its support of laws and unions that help the working class improve wages and benefits and ensures an individuals rights to work in a safe environment. Republican efforts have consistently been against workers rights, unions or anything that would impinge on corporate freedom to have it their way.

Go back two hundred years(200) and take a look at capitalist's demands on workers. The start of the Textile Revolution, if not the total American Industrial Revolution, began in New England, where we grew up and where some of you still live in Massachusetts. Capitalists built the entire city of Lowell around textile mills. They dammed the Merrimack River, built canals across miles of the country side, laid trolley car tracks connecting outlying towns to get workers into the mills, constructed "mill girl houses" for the thousands of women immigrants being brought to this country to work in the mills. They built factory after factory, until the famous Mile of Mills was finished.

Years later, it became one of the first outsourcing projects that moved an entire industry, in America. The textile industry was moved from New England to our southern states, where wages were lower. Some of what remains of the Mile of Mills in Lowell, Mass, is now the site of the National Textile Museum. Capitalists have not changed, they want your efforts to create more capital, end of story. My definition of capital, "money earned by someone else, to put in a rich person's pocket." That definition may not be what's in the dictionary, but it is what happens in the real world.

If you are a worker, employed to make or do something, if the natural resource and your effort are not rich enough to be turned into a profit to create wealth, both are abandoned, EVEN if it helped our society. If you cannot make the process you are employed in create more wealth for the business, they make you work longer for the same pay, fire you-hire someone else for less pay, cut benefits or have another company do the job. We have seen it all. Many large corporations, in many countries including America, will opt for having the work done elsewhere before trying to re-educate workers they already have. These same workers, some with 20 and

30 years of dedicated and productive work for the company, are simply discarded like a soiled paper towel. They are one and the same people who helped the company accumulate their wealth, the technology, and the foundation to continue and prosper.

Outsourcing has been in America as long as there have been people called capitalists. America was built on capitalism and it is great when there is a reasonable return to the worker, for the work they accomplish. Capitalists are very often seen as the bad guys. Maybe that's because there are more than a fair share of them who care about NOTHING but the bottom line. What is paramount however, is how capitalism is used.

How do the companies generating the new capital compensate workers? What does the company do to make certain the workers health is protected? What procedures do they use to protect the environment? How do they make sure a natural resource is not being destroyed just so they can make more profit? Is the generation of this new capital going to benefit society or just the few people at the top?

The period after World War II was when the American workers made real progress, many achieving the American Dream. Middle class America emerged in full bloom. Democrats joined together to pass laws to improve workers pay and mandate safe working conditions, in the face of stiff opposition from Republican politicians.

- MINIMUM WAGE
- 40 HOUR WEEK
- OVERTIME PAY AFTER NORMAL WORK HOURS
- SAFE WORKING CONDITIONS - OSHA
- HEALTH CARE
- DEFINED BENEFIT PENSIONS
- WORKER DISABILITY ASSISTANCE
- HOLIDAYS, VACATIONS, MATERNITY LEAVE, SICK LEAVE

You name it, Democrats made it happen for the workers, Republicans fought it tooth and nail. UNIONS were in the lead, achieving increases in pay, health care and pensions. Spillover from the gains of the unions were felt by non-union workers, increased wages and benefits were reluctantly provided by big business, to prevent the spread of the union movement. Stopping unions is still of paramount importance, today, for Republicans, supported by corporations.

There were many men of great distinction, with inventive genius and foresight that emerged during the 1900's. Many created products that brought us into the ever changing world of computers, and the tools that have transformed and continue to transform society today. Many of these individuals created capital by employing workers who were paid reasonable wages and benefits. Both the capitalists and the workers prospered. Capitalists who create jobs that pay a living wage, are few and far between today.

CORPORATE RULES ON HOW TO TREAT WORKERS

Have we turned the calendar back? Hire workers as cheap as you can, pay them as little as possible, work them as long as they can stand up, damn the environment and worker safety. There are no laws saying we have to treat workers like they are humans. Those were the corporate rules during the start of the 19th century in America. Those are the rules in the developing nations today, the 21st century. The basic difference is that in America during the 1800's corporations set the conditions for labor, while the government turned its back on individual rights. Now it is the governments that sets the conditions for labor, while the capitalists turn their head, so they will not be accused of using slave labor. All the rights of workers are ignored by these governments and the corporations using them to produce their products, especially COMMUNIST CHINA.

They do not believe anyone, except the government, has RIGHTS. And government's rights are supreme, above anything you may want to discuss. Just look at the Chinese record since the Communist revolution succeeded in 1949. Look, but don't be surprised if there are large gaps or revised historical "facts". Communist governments do not allow black marks to be noted that would cast any shadow on their government because theirs is a record of cruelty and brutal oppression.

Corporations from all countries around the world are sending jobs of every description to China. When we complain about working the poor people like slaves, the comeback is always "they are better off than they were, working in the fields". May be, but it does not give anyone the right to exploit human beings. These people are not given a choice. They are assigned to a factory, told what job they will do, when they will do it and how much money they will make. They may live in barracks, away from their family, work six days a week, have 2 or 3 holidays and a week off for Chinese New Year, to visit their families. That was normal 20 years ago, it has improved with the communist/capitalist movement, but who are the people that are benefiting, do you have to be a communist PARTY member to reap the real gains?

This great country of ours, our President George W. Bush, our corporate leaders, politicians of every party, Democrat, Republican, Independent, whatever, have no problem sending 90% of American manufacturing and production to a Communist country where everything is owned by the communist government (including people), controlled by the communist government and planned by the communist government.

The communist leaders make or break laws as they see fit, allow other peoples inventions to be used without compensation, and they assume intellectual property protection does not exist. They do not allow any serious religious movement, except a token church here and there, to provide an appearance of religious freedom, treat dissidents with swift and harsh punishment, it is common if they are never seen again and they exemplify a cruel Communist government. Is that what the Republicans are turning our country into? They are certainly trying, based on past performance.

Of course, Communist China is willing to take, yes we are giving it to them, our technology and everything else necessary to dominate the world. George W. Bush, Republican President of the these United States, allows corporate America to give away our most valuable asset to the archenemy of capitalism, our manufacturing capability, so corporations can make a bigger profit, while destroying our economy.

China is a large communist country, roughly the same geographical size as the USA. They have subsisted on meager diets for centuries and it is with communism that they have provided most people enough food, at least so they will not starve. Whether they work in the fields, a mine or a factory, their pay by American standards is chump change. The pay of ten(10) workers in China does not come close to the pay of one(1) living wage worker in America. So you see the eyes of capitalists light up, when they can BUY workers at such a low pay level.

I said communism is what allowed the Chinese to feed most of their people. While that is true, communism was fatal to 10's of millions of people who were slaughtered in the transition to communism, while free countries did nothing. The most common misnomer about communism, is that everyone works together. In fact, it is exactly the opposite, what little people have, they fiercely protect. Most will not lend a helping hand to anyone. The perception that they work together is completely wrong. Everyone is for themselves. They will snitch to the authorities on their mother or their brother, if they can PERCEIVE a personal gain. They are like we have become in America, worried only about ourselves.

Campaign rhetoric is in full swing. Messages used over and over, to make people hear it often enough so they begin to think it's true. There are professional writers, for both Republican and Democratic parties, who use every resource available to come up with speeches and phrases to catch your attention, 99% of what they say is either an outright lie or it cannot be achieved in your lifetime. The remaining 1% is most likely a half-truth. During this election process they will spend a new record for Presidential campaigns. How many hundred's of millions of dollars will be poured down the media drain, in the 2008 presidential race? It is astronomical. With the amount of money being used to get their message heard, you could sell snowballs to people in Alaska. For the past 50 or so years, it has been the party with the most money that wins elections. In most of the last 30 years Republicans have raised much more than Democrats. There have been a few cases where money did not get a person elected, but it is rare and most likely other resources were lacking. Support has to come from the local, state and national levels.

Republican politicians rely heavily on big business. As this election cycle starts getting down to the final candidates, big business will support the Republican nominee, with millions of dollars, no matter who it is or what their background may be, as long as they say they are Republican.

Unions are casualties of the Republican Administrations and corporations, continually chipping away at wages and benefits of union workers, where they "buy" the living wage workers into retirement, making way for new LOWER paid workers. With unions at their weakest point in 50 years, they cannot win any battles to improve a working persons status. As a result a new wage structure has been created, dragging down all American workers standards, much of the present problem starting with that great Republican hero(myth), Ronald Reagan. But we have covered that sad period for working families earlier.

Where will the decrease in wages end, without unions to fight against the Republicans and the insensitive corporations? We are in for a very disturbing decline, major corporations are pulling all wages below any reasonable standard, and we are allowing them to do it. In the case of one of the best and strongest unions in the nation, the unions were forced to agree to retire older well paid workers, then they allowed the replacement workers to be paid at rates that are one half in some cases and that are not a living wage. Instead of our standard of living going up, like it had been before a 16 year reign of immoral, corrupt Republican administrations, 8 Reagan, 8 Bush, it is going down. Now, no one may be able to reverse the process of American workers being fed to the wolves by corrupt corporations.

Here is where the Democratic, Independent, and various other political party members loose their way. They will vote for someone of a different political party who has an idea that they like, a position they consider important or a promise to fight for a program they consider important, to them. Regardless of what prior facts are, enough lies, enough times, what people perceive to be correct, can be changed. That is how politics works, in America. That may be democracy, but it is also how minorities, like Republicans, end up ruling majorities, like Democrats; overwhelming rhetoric, lies, "facts" that are true for 300 people and they extrapolate them for

300 million to make their distortions seem real. And Republicans do it well. So if you are a union member or any worker, and you want to express how you feel about a candidate, because they promise the world and beyond, remember that promises politicians make are broken, at any time they feel it will be to their advantage. They will break their pledge to the public before they cross the line and "vote with the other party." It is almost as rare as hen's teeth, they will never vote against their party, even if it would be for the common good of everyone.

To my children;

Democracy is a great thing. We have the right to vote for who we want and for what party we want. But democracy also comes with obligations. We have to make sure our vote will count towards the things that make our society the best place, for a working person(the majority), in the world. We are experiencing the worst conditions for unions in the past 50 years. For anyone who has to work for a living, like in manufacturing, the trades or the service groups, wages continue to go down while inflation goes up. That is making a very significant impact on our lives. If we continue on this path of decreasing wages, we will soon have two classes, like they do in underdeveloped countries, the rich and the poor. And I know where I will be!

We need to THINK when we vote, who do your favorite politicians represent, you or the political and corporate forces against the workers of America? A simple search on the internet will show you how they have voted in the past, their votes in the future will follow the same pattern, regardless of their promises to do otherwise. Republicans have never voted for major legislation that would promote workers benefits or help the working person. It has not happened in my lifetime, it will not happen in the future.

Stay healthy, be happy and be kind,

Love,

Dad/Grandpa.

XXXXXXXXXX X2

LETTER 11

ARE WE REALLY ALL AMERICANS?

Hi everyone;

There was a time about 50 years ago, when Americans were considered reasonable people and were respected, like anyone else on our planet. Traveling to England, Germany, France, even Mexico and Taiwan, was a pleasure and you could expect to receive a reasonable reception from the people who lived there. We have changed to a society that no longer reflects what was considered AMERICAN values, where people take into account others, when they are going about their daily lives. Twenty years or so later, the phrase "the ugly American" started to raise its head, the indication Americans were losing their respect for other people, respect is returned when given. Today, every American is out for themselves, it starts at the top and works its way down. It has progressed to where you need someone to "cover your back" in everything you do. Is this the American society we worked for?

Now we have a new and menacing threat to all Americans, a life changing problem for every working person in America, the new world economy. And unless we bring back the philosophy that as Americans we will lend a hand to each other, we are going to lose the all important battle of preserving a middle class. This new world economy puts all American workers at great risk, especially when corporations have acted ANTI-AMERICAN. Politicians and many others in our society have lost sight of the impending assault on our workers. We should be talking about new job initiatives, how to save our working families with training and retraining, save their homes by protecting them from predatory lenders, and how to PROTECT AMERICA, security is at it's lowest point in fifty years. A Republican misnomer, "we will make you safer".

Jobs have been disappearing for years, but many were too technical, or at least we thought so, to be outsourced. Computer software development comes to mind, once very much dominated by companies in America. Now Microsoft has built the largest software development center in the world, in COMMUNIST CHINA. How long will it take for them to have every secret - industrial, military and financial, at their disposal. Isn't that a SECURITY RISK of national proportions? What does our National Security Council have to say about that? It is OK if we do it for business purposes? "American security at risk, from a COMMUNIST country, not a chance. Its al Qaeda we need to crush, not communism. "Who, what, run that by me again, someone has been brainwashed!" Or is it like every other government office, there is NO one available to check, they have reports to write about how great a job they are doing, protecting us.

Republicans tout that keeping America safe, is most important and it is their superiority over the Democrats in that regard that makes them qualified to lead our country. What are we being kept safe from, finding out the capitalists are in a full-blown effort to sell America while Republicans continue to give them all the support they need to make it happen? What part of that is called AMERICAN? What AMERICAN would do such a thing?

Are we building a fence to cover the fact that we are now less secure than at any time in recent history? Or to divert our attention from the fact that the fence will have a superhighway going thru it, bringing goods from the new super-sized ports being built in Mexico, so they can bypass the American UNIONS in American PORTS, an outsourcing tragedy of immense proportions for American longshoremen, our port workers. Will the trucks on the superhighway bypass all the import checks that are supposed to happen, but never do, just like our ports of entry do today? Or will the super-sized ports be under COMMUNIST CHINA control, the same people now building these ports in Mexico. Their products do not need controls, everything is perfect, "like toys with lead paint for our kids". So much for American SECURITY, of any kind. We have Republican President George Bush engaging in "progressive talks" with Mexico and Canada to ensure there will be a free flow of goods on this highway. Is that for AMERICAN INTERESTS? It may be if we talk about North and South America, but certainly it is not good for the United States of America, we will lose 100's of millions of dollars and leave thousands more American workers, including our longshoremen, without jobs. Lets hope we can change course at the next election, before every job is sold by this Republican Administration.

We are in for a surprise, we thought some jobs were untouchable, we could not outsource them. Now very job in America, except hands on service type jobs, is being outsourced. Remember the radiologists in India that I mentioned, who are performing analysis for doctors in this USA. If they can outsource medical doctors, you had better hold onto your hats, things are moving very quickly and your nice high paying job may vanish overnight, if your NOT very American corporation finds someone, anywhere, cheaper, to do the work. This Republican/capitalist administration has done nothing to alleviate or mitigate the outsourcing of jobs. Are they representing and considering American workers when they shut down factories, or is their commitment now to foreign governments, like Communist China. China must have changed completely, from COMMUNIST TO CAPITALIST in 20 years? The fact is that they have NOT changed. It is impossible for me to believe, and their government has not change their name or their ways. More fairy tails about being AMERICAN, you cannot be when you ship everything to China!

In earlier times, outsourcing was done with some consideration and concern for the workers being displaced. Today corporations abandon their workers without any ramifications whatsoever. Are these American corporations, or corporations that WERE American, now under foreign control. It would seem to me that if they were American, they would not be using the errant excuse of the bottom line, as the only criteria for outsourcing EVERY American job.

Is providing healthcare for children, they are America's FUTURE and there is nothing more AMERICAN, a national priority? Only hot dogs and apple pie come close. You would expect it would be from any responsible person in America. Our Republican President asks congress for $180 Billion for the war one day, then vetoes a bill the next day that provides $7 billion more a year to maintain and expand child healthcare so additional AMERICAN families would be eligible. Do you remember the Republicans shouting "We are for Family Values"? How about demonstrating something that supports that claim, you may want to try the American way, provide living wage jobs, so they do not need assistance to live a normal American LIFE. No, Virginia, it is sad to say, but American corporations and Republican politicians are not interested in preserving the American way of life, it must have been a dream. Our Republican President VETOED KIDS healthcare. Republican congress men and women also voted against kids healthcare, they upheld his veto. That is NOT being American in my mind. He is going to show the nation, that he is still relevant, He is the boss. What hypocrites this President and his Republican supporters are.

These same people also claim to be Pro Life, but they will not provide healthcare for children? It's way beyond being hypocrites, way beyond being un-American, it's evil.

That is not being disrespectful of the Presidency, it is being truthful, something sorely lacking in America these days. He can veto a $7 billion increase for child healthcare in America, then ask for hundreds of billions for the WAR in Iraq. What America do they support? Is that an American president? Are our representatives American, sent to Washington to help American children? Are kids creating this problem, or is it a President acting like a kid? Kids are not that evil, but we are doing our best to get them there.

President Bush is supported by about 200 Republican congressional lawmakers, in the body that writes the spending bills, in congress. We have seen time and again how these 200 people, who are supposed to be representing all the people of America, uphold a presidential veto, even when the majority of Americans want the bill passed. Imagine 200 people, against millions that mirror the will of the majority of Americans, and those 200 other guys win. What a national disgrace! They do not reflect American VALUES.

President Bush and his Republican supporters, have permanently damaged America and its standing in the world. By invading Iraq and continuing the slaughter for years, they may be making it impossible for the workers of America(if there are any left), to climb their way out of this financial and moral morass. We cannot let politicians and the current crop of capitalists destroy us. Lets wake up, be true AMERICANS, take our country back before it is too late.

We have seen the arrogance displayed by Republican lawmakers, as they have usurped the right that belongs to all Americans, that of being able to determine the future of our country. Has the industrial/military complex that supports the Republican agenda, or vice-versa, been taken over by foreign governments, like much of Wall Street and the "American" financial institutions? Is that why there is not a scintilla of concern by the CEO's, when company after company leaves its workers high and dry? That is not what real American companies have been known to do. I remember when AMERICAN corporations treated its workers fairly, when they no longer needed their services, they helped them find new employment. But of course that is the problem, there are no other places for a manufacturing production worker to find employment, it is a desperate situation for most American workers. We need to stop the bleeding of America NOW!

We are fighting the battle of our lives, we need to put America first, like TRUE Americans would.

Then they feed us lies about the condition of our economy, giving workers false hope. Do you see any worker retraining programs that will fill our massive jobs void, created by the latest and greatest round of manufacturing outsourcing? It is not something we can stop, but we can PLAN for America's FUTURE. Or is that at too high an intellectual level for this President and his Cabinet?

We are being fed lies about why our wages are going down. They say it is unions, illegal aliens and healthcare costs that are to blame. It is none of those, it is IMPORTING everything we consume, without any control whatsoever of those imports. We are being fed lies about inflation, when the cost of every food item has gone up, sometimes 50% or more in a single year. Gasoline is over $3.00 a gallon. Of course the government computes inflation at 2% or 3%. Yet another un-AMERICAN joke.

Many potential solutions to our energy crisis were available, rejected by the capitalists and others as "not economically viable", environmentalists as our doomsayers, or by the foolhardy people with the "not in my back yard" syndrome. Every option of sustainable energy must be considered, if they are truly sustainable they should be environmentally friendly and must be explored.

The Republicans are right when they rail against the Democrats, that we have too much big government. What they don't say is they are the major contributor. Isn't that hypocritical or have they coined another phrase for dishonesty? During the Republican Reagan administration, the government grew by 300,000 jobs. What the record will be for this REPUBLICAN Bush administration remains to be seen but it looks like a repeat. Most likely the private sector will have assumed lucrative government activities, leaving any mess for the Democrats to clean up. No signs of real AMERICAN leaders, we are on our own. Where are the retraining programs for the millions of discarded American workers? Our Democracy is sinking, our economy is crippled, the lenders are cashing in their chips, TRUE AMERICAN leaders, where are you?

HOME OWNERSHIP.

The last time that I remember people losing their homes in great numbers, was what I read about in the GREAT DEPRESSION of the 1930's. While I lived during that period as a child, it is not something I remember very much about. This Republican Administration has enough Republican members in congress to block any effective legislation to help the homeowners, they help everyone else, not America's HOMEOWNERS? It looks very, very distressing to me.

We have the mortgage predators on Wall Street, who have significantly damaged our economy by increasing interest rates to the levels that are usury, a crime, by legal definition, but not in the eyes of a Republican. Many workers are losing their homes, even if they did not lose their jobs, their monthly mortgage increases of hundreds of dollars, because of "interest adjustments". To translate that, it means so called private enterprise, which is now more like FOREIGN COUNTRIES, needs the money. Mortgages were bundled and sold to make billions of dollars for international investors, another group without a conscience. By the looks of things there is no bottom in sight. One of the most significant items of the American Dream, owning your own home, has been sold by the Republicans, via Wall Street scalpers. To China? Saudi Arabia? The Arab Emirates? Home ownership, under this Bush Republican Administration, has been flushed down the toilet, over 1,000,000 homes lost already, and we are just starting in 2008. A typical Republican action, tuck it to the little guy.

LEGAL IMMIGRANTS

Our country was built by LEGAL and ILLEGAL immigrants. There will always be some who will come to America, at any cost. Legal immigrants are always welcome in America. But if we grant amnesty to 20 million illegal aliens who have broken the law to get here, will we also grant amnesty to the million or more of our citizens we have jailed for a crime of similar seriousness. Some AMERICAN citizens are serving long "mandatory" jail sentences for dealing with ounces of drugs. Illegal aliens carry many pounds of drugs across our border every day. Will we also give our imprisoned American citizens amnesty? Will we commute that "mandatory sentence" for our citizens, like we want to do for illegal alien law breakers? If our citizens in prison promise to pay a fine, take a course in understanding the law, and wait in line like the illegal aliens, will that satisfy their prison sentence?

We talk about immigration like it is destroying America. It is not, and will not. The real threat to our living wage jobs is cargo ship after cargo ship bringing products here, the same products that we once exported. Cheaper goods, being made with slave labor, and Americans gobble them up. By eating the imported food, watching the imported TV, on our imported furniture, in a home built with imported materials, delivered by an imported truck, we are consuming every AMERICAN JOB, maybe even our own. We are getting to the bottom of the barrel, the time for action has passed. We better change before the barrel is empty. Will we go from a great recession, to a great DEPRESSION?

AMERICA'S RACE WAR.

When everything else has been discussed concerning the question, are we REALLY all Americans, we come to the most deep rooted American prejudice, the color of a persons skin, the only thing that divides our society beyond any logical reasoning. It would be safe to say that America has been built, literally, by people from every race, from every country around the globe. Often those who did the building, did not do so because it was America the beautiful that they were working for, it was capitalists that brought them here, very often by force but America was the place to be, when they needed labor to complete many difficult tasks, "that Americans did not want to do". That phrase was probably used 200 years ago, as justification to bring many people from Africa to work in the fields. Sound familiar? Quite a familiar phrase 200 years later. There were the Chinese to work on the railroads, the Irish and Scotch to work in the textile mills, and a myriad of others who were brought here by the capitalists or who came here on their on volition, to pick up the gold, that they were told, lined the streets. All these people would become the foundation for our American society. Their ancestors, you and me, are now free to do what we want, where we want, when we want, a great legacy for those workers, who became AMERICAN workers. Every person, all skin colors, from every nation, have been assimilated into our society. Yet we cannot seem to get over the negative opinions of the skin color of our ancestors, the same people who built America, especially if it is brown or as some prefer, black. If we look at the ancestral origin of every person in America, there will be few who are considered to be "pure blooded" anything, only American.

Nowhere will you find that skin color has anything to do with the character of the individual. We can say without reservation that any race is inherently as good as any other. It has been proven again and again, color is only skin deep when it comes to character and the desire to achieve, it may be significant for certain physical traits and medical issues, but not for the desire to be an AMERICAN.

If we consider the racial makeup of most Americans, we should understand that everyone has very distant relatives of many origins, including black. Many of our ancestors are from Europe, where countries were over-run by people from every other nation, depending on who felt the most powerful at the time. The bloodlines of the conquered people did not stay pure anything, they were mingled with the conquerors. Think about the immigrants from and into the Mediterranean countries , Italy, Greece, Spain, all of them, to believe that there is not a drop of blood from racially intermingled bloodlines is absurd and unrealistic, no matter what anyone says. We know and readily accept the mix of oriental and white people, the combinations of just about every nationality, but we have a deep profound prejudice for anyone mixed with brown(black) and in many cases for brown itself.

Is mixing the black race with the white race(how white, most people do not know or care about) something that is degrading to our society? Is it like mixing paint, once you put in black it cannot be called white, it is off-white, but never white. Shouldn't it be some shade of white, it most certainly is NOT BLACK. Why is a racial mixed child born to a black mother and a white father, or vice versa, called black. This child is one half white and one half black, a 50-50 gene pool from the parents. Why are they automatically called black, not white? They can claim to be just as white as they are black, and in many other cases they are more white than black, but they call themselves black, or others do. Is it they want to be "not-white". A truly discouraging phenomena that has to be rejected in this 21st century, when it is used for negative purposes. Lets be REAL AMERICANS, discard the racial bigotry, treat everyone like you want to be treated. With respect.

It has taken a long time to bring our society to where it is "almost mature". We need to take the next step and come together, everyone as AMERICANS, not black American, African American, Italian American or Irish American. Those are fine names for cultural or family issues, but not when referring to the people of our nation, where all colors have given their lives to protect AMERICA and are doing it today. If individuals or groups want to be associated with black heritage, why do they call themselves African Americans instead of the way it should be, American Africans? Is that to show they want to be something else first, American second? It goes the same for people of all nationalities that live in America, put American first. The best country in the world deserves it.

When we consider heritage we should be looking at the positive aspects of our ancestors, they made our land, AMERICA, what it is, the best place in the world. We cannot continue the divisive, ANTI-AMERICAN policies we have pursued. We must get with it, be REAL Americans, throw out partisan politics, be one, the American Party.

Religious bigotry, social injustice, political skullduggery, racial intolerance, are by themselves intolerable, we need to concentrate on how we will remain AMERICAN, a name above all others, a great name to be proud of.

To My Children;

Elections are coming. We need to decide if we want to stop this decay of our lifestyle, or proceed with politics as usual. Continuing on this Republican path will be an economic death sentence for many AMERICANS. We continue to "play politics" while the rest of the world is leaving us in the dust, it is the dust from the capitalists, as they head out of town with all of AMERICA'S technology. They WERE American capitalists, now their allegiance is to COMMUNIST and other countries. Set aside Democrat, Republican, Whatever, and be AMERICANS, with one goal in mind, return to a democracy that is by the people, just like the word democracy means. Racial prejudice, must be replaced with logical, not emotional thinking, it is just plain stupid. Lets start thinking and acting like we are serious about wanting to insure that every child's future will be healthy, prosperous, and safe, in AMERICA.

Stay healthy, be happy and be kind,

Love,
Dad/Grandpa
XXXXXXXXXX X2

LETTER 12

PESSIMIST OR *REALIST*

Hi everyone;

Well, this is my last letter for a while, and at 75 years old, who knows what "a while" will bring. Most of my letters have been asking questions, not providing answers, like an elder is supposed to do. But that is what everyone should be doing, asking questions, are we doing the right things for our country and the future, for all children? At this time, I believe we are failing miserably, by all or any account. I see our country heading downhill, at 100 miles an hour, without a steering wheel.

Many of my comments may seem pessimistic, but they are my candid view of how we are being sold down the river by our government and our capitalist "friends". For 60 years, I have observed how workers in America have risen to a great middle class, to become the essence of our society. Home ownership, educating our children, reasonable healthcare, good working conditions, vacations, a promise of retirement,

all these things came to those who worked hard, were honest and strived to help their EMPLOYER succeed, where everyone prospers in the process. But all that has changed, because of LIES of our government and corporations, especially the Republican Party who supports corporate "America", and because of ourselves, our disrespect for others and a we want it all attitude, and we want it now.

For the last 7 years we have seen the decimation of working people accelerate beyond belief. It is most discouraging to see the dismay of hard working people, being told it is the end of the line, when they have 10 or 12 years to retirement. "You have been replaced, by a worker in India(or China or Indonesia)." Or a young person out of school hearing, "most of that type of work has been outsourced to Poland." And we thought we were going to work for American companies, who should have some loyalty to the workers that made them successful or who we expected to put "American workers first". We have ourselves to blame, we have become selfish, without respect for anything or anyone, a throw away society. The problem is that we are throwing away our future, the present living wage American workers are the first casualty. We are not willing to do things that might get our hands dirty, or take up some of our leisure time. Shame on us. Goods built by sweat shops, Communist China, Communist anything, or any company or country that effectively has "sweat shop labor," should be banned from our ports. But we will not do it, we have no backbone or gumption to stand up to the capitalists and our Republican government who have betrayed us. We can stop the economic carnage ourselves, stop buying imported products. We could, but we will not, we do not have the guts!

Do we think we can continue consuming cheap goods, built with pennies per hour labor, and have our wages go up and our economy boom? Only a fool would think we can do that, and it appears we have been fools. How long can we import everything we use, building up trade deficits we cannot even count, causing the decline of the dollar, before we have given away our future? Has it happened already? Its not looking good.

Our economy looks more grim than my letters. Do we think that capitalists are going to change their ways and become loyal employers again? It will never happen. Everyone is convinced-by political deceit, that it is the workers coming across the Mexican border who are lowering our wages and taking our jobs.

Let me repeat, while illegal aliens are causing many cities and states great harm, it is nothing compared to the uncontrolled imports, on a sea train of cargo ships, bringing goods that never stop flowing off these ships, that is the REAL problem. When you add the 100's of billions of barrels, that's trillions of gallons, of oil we import, our southern border is inconsequential, not even close to being our real problem. That is with the exception of the DRUG trade, where each individual, every American is RESPONSIBLE for this problem. IF Americans didn't use the illicit drugs, we wouldn't have a drug problem, but we cannot take the blame ourselves, can we, its not me - it's the drug smugglers.

Our economic DEMISE is coming into our ports legally, from much further away than Mexico. Politicians keep the light shining on something they say is being "fixed", by a fence, it keeps us happy and the corrupt in power. Did you ever have a dog that will not stay restrained? You put up a fence and he digs under it or jumps over it. Nothing will keep him in, short of providing what he really needs. When you provide what he needs, you may not need the fence for him to stay in his own back yard. Maybe we should look at the source of the problem. With the billions of dollars to build a fence, then spend more millions on a continuing basis to patrol the border, could this money be better spent on helping Mexico provide better jobs? Or is it another case of too much corruption, on both sides of the fence?

Those cargo ships I mentioned, coming into our ports, are the equivalent of virtual workers from India, China and elsewhere, coming ashore with every trailer load of goods. Each trailer has a worker, coming ashore in our ports, legally walking down the street, to KICK YOU OUT of your job. It is essentially no different than our southern border, except there are 100 times as many and they are legal, coming in the form of IMPORTED products. When we consider the continuous flow of goods and oil into our country, the corrupt corporations, our criminally corrupt government, we are indeed, no questions asked, in trouble. How we got here may be subject to lengthy debate, but there is little time for that. Solutions, your ideas, of how to correct the ways of the greatest country in the world gone bad, are needed now. Our country has been brought to its knees, a bad place to start a fight for our economic viability, immediate action is desperately needed.

I consider my thoughts and ideas to be REALISTIC, but the people who run our country and their supporters, will dismiss me as something else, not to be mentioned when children are present. I have lived 75 years in the best country in the world, and I want our country to stay that way for all children in the future.

When I started writing these letters several months ago, it was with the idea of trying to explain "what went wrong and how my children were left with an emotional minefield." After half a dozen tries, and thinking about all the unethical actions of our so called leaders and the economic problems we are facing, it seemed I was again doing the wrong thing, trying to correct the past. It is our children's future that is at stake, as always the case, the past cannot be erased, and saying you are sorry does not do much. Every decision you make in your lifetime, will become part of you, in some way. While most of our actions go unnoticed when we do them, they are there and when least expected, they will come back and you will say, "I am glad I did that" or conversely, "I am sorry I did that". We have to hope that glad outweigh the sorry when we are through with our lives, and that time comes a lot sooner than you think. With all the negative forces out to destroy America, it is more important than ever to make the right choices, like I am glad I did that.

To address those who may think I am a pessimist , a few additional facts may help to dispel that notion. As an optimist, I was able to change my life from a granite quarry worker, to achieving significant positions as an engineer in the corporate world and as an entrepreneur in private enterprise. That could not be achieved, as a pessimist. My pay was always good, a direct result of education, hard work, and very important - LUCK. Luck, at least my definition, is being willing to work long and hard, accept responsibility and challenges, and communicate with your peers. Accepting responsibility does not mean the Bush variety, "You mean that is what I said, it must be a mistake, we will ignore it, those are just the facts".

I have been able to re-start my life several times; after divorce, having a business fail, losing a home, and having the Communist Chinese government sabotage a successful, functioning, computer joint venture company in China, while I was the plant manager. The joint venture was to manufacture personal computers, PCs, but the Chinese government wanted main frame computers. President Reagan and his administration would not allow such sophisticated technology to be exported to a communist country, it was a security risk. Even traveling to Communist China may jeopardize a persons ability to receive a security clearance, necessary for many jobs in the computer industry.

George Bush and his administration would not know what a security risk was if it was stamped all over it in red letters. Not only that, he would change the security classification, like he did in the Libby case, if he felt like it. Security, is that with a capital S? Main frames, as we knew them, are now relics, but the technology that made American computers world class have proven invaluable to the world. That decision by the Communist government proved to be poorly timed, a multimillion dollar project scuttled by Communist party bureaucrats. It turned out that the only main frame computer maker to survive the great main frame meltdown in the late 80's was IBM. All the other companies and there were several with sales in the billions of dollars, went out of business. The PC that we had introduced in China, became the new computer system for the next millennium. Another instance where I had to be an optimist to continue, having a serious stroke at 72 years old and working everyday since then to recover. So you can call me anything, but not a pessimist.

To look at why my letters have many disparaging statements, we have to look at our society and review the results of the last few years of a criminal administration. Capitalist betrayals, government corruption, religious scandals, a medical system that works for the rich, an economy slipping deeper into recession,(depression?) each day,

failing schools-by any industrialized country standards, people losing their homes in numbers not seen since the great depression of the 1930's. Living wage jobs have been eliminated by every corporation that was once an American corporation, now mostly owned by international investors, including Communist and Arab governments. And this is America?

We have a war, started by our government, who proclaim they are Christians, against another country because a group of religious fanatics attacked and killed some of our citizens. They are a faction of the Muslim religion. Have we gone back 1000 years to religious wars? Their fanatical sect attacked us! Is it a Christian response-kill them?

Or the negligent behavior, seen over and over, of how we treat the elderly and the less fortunate. Failing to care for millions of our people, 50 million people without healthcare. And this is America?

Poor people who are malnourished, do not have healthcare or medications, they are poorly educated, will live in poverty with their lives shortened by our callous disregard for people less fortunate than ourselves. And this is America?

Isn't it time for some common sense, and empathy for those who need help? Everyone cannot care for themselves, no matter what the Republicans say. Programs to help the disadvantaged break the vicious cycle of poverty are necessary. It ends up costing everyone to care for a family when the father cannot find a job, so put them to work, the differential of welfare or workfare will be small in dollars, enormous knowing it means you are caring for your family. Many programs have been tried, countless times, with very limited success, maybe it will succeed this time.

I have mentioned Communist China a lot in my letters, and how we have sent all our manufacturing capability there. Does anyone remember the Korean conflict, and how America could not defeat a small, 3rd world country? We settled for a truce, half of the country free to choose, the other half communist, Korea remains a thorn in our side, everyday. Did you ever ask why we could not defeat the Korean communists? Their neighbors on the north and good communist allies, Russia and China, perhaps? Is China a new Communist ally for Democracy? Are you serious? Is it another George Bush fiasco, like our "good friends" the Russians?

What about Vietnam? Why couldn't we defeat the communists in Vietnam, another 3rd word country, that should have been no competition for our excellent armed forces? Again, their neighbors on the north and communist allies, Russia and China, perhaps? But some seem to think that communism is dead, as several politicians, like idiots, have stated. One third of the world is under the control of communism, whether they pretend to be capitalists or not. They do not intend to end their march anytime soon, as we can see in South America, Africa, Cuba and just about everywhere around the globe. We have a war in Afghanistan, a war in Iraq, a war on our Mexican border, a war on the middle class, and the forgotten war on drugs. Another failed war in our own back yard.

Why did we fail and why do we continue to let drugs destroy our people and our society? Because America IS the largest market, for illegal drugs in the world. We, that includes everyone, have to decide when enough is enough. Evidently the American people are going to let the sale of drugs continue unabated. With drugs being sold in the amounts we have in this country, it is only possible for this to go on if people at very high levels, allow drugs to be sold in every city and town in the country. It cannot happen without collusion of some authorities, it is too massive an undertaking. We see it every day. The local drug dealer gets busted, sent to prison, but the source of the drugs does not stop. Once in a while we have a "big" bust, some major players are sent to prison. But then they are allowed to continue their drug activities from their prison cells, where our prisons become a drug dealers sanctuary.

Is it fear? Are the drug dealers too aggressive, with a kill or be killed attitude? Are they too powerful to overcome? Or is it greed? Where authorities get some of the action for themselves, by looking the other way or enabling the dealers? In many countries they solve the problem quickly, they execute drug dealers, and not after 20 years of legal wrangling, it happens very quickly, often in days, maybe weeks. Our capitalists favorite, the Chinese Government, wastes little time before it kills a drug dealer, and they may do it with a public execution.

Capitalists control every commodity in the world. Wheat, corn, gold, diamonds, precious metals and even pork bellies. Why can't they control the commodities that produce drugs? Or do they? If we bought every bale of coca leaves in South America, all the poppy bulbs from the farmers in Afghanistan and made "recreational drugs" legal so they could be controlled, it would cost one thousandth of what we spend on trying to prevent distribution, doing drug investigations, drug busts, incarcerating druggies and the dealers, and footing the cost of crime that follows in the devastation of drugs. From the beginning to the end, drugs especially hurts families of the addicted. But we never get the big players, the deals must go on.

It cannot be done you say. We have had some Afghan farmers plant other crops, but they produced crops that had far less cash return than the poppy crop. Then we wonder why they go back to their big money plant that produces a much better cash return and is ultimately turned into a cash cow, heroin. Isn't that the Republicans philosophy of doing business? Get what you can, as long as you can make a profit. For the farmer producing the poppies, it is not a moral issue, he is simply trying to survive. It is the middle man, the drug dealer, the man with the money(the capitalist), who is converting the product into illegal drugs.

Coca is somewhat different in that it is used for cultural and medicinal purposes in most South American countries, in addition to selling it for dugs. But there has to be a way, the drug dealers do it, are they smarter than we are? Or is it fear, drug lords and drug dealers will KILL anyone they consider a threat to their multi-billion dollar business, even law enforcement officers and government officials are not off limits to drug dealers.

It is time to treat them with the same response. Use our military to wipe them out. Period.

Make it harsh and swift, like addiction initially does to its victims. Unfortunately, an addicts suffering goes on until someone, hopefully themselves, or something can break the addiction, impossible for some to do without significant intervention.

IRAQ

Today we still have the ill-fated war in Iraq, killing our brave men and women, and we have the same chances of "winning" as we did in Korea and Vietnam. A war started by our criminal administration, who cared nothing about the negative impact of the superpower destroying a small sovereign country. The goal was to force a regime change, depose Saddam Hussein. Well our military completed the job in about 4 weeks. We should have come out of Iraq at that time with the flags of victory waving. We won, but our criminal administration blew it. This Republican President and his incompetent appointees changed the goal:

Nation building. Build a Democracy in Iraq, so George Bush can have something to call his "legacy." In the process they sent every aspect of the Iraqi country into chaos and a civil war. Everyone with an ounce of brains, including the military, agreed we should not be involved in their civil war WE created, we should have withdrawn our troops. But no, we did not. So they changed the goal.

We cannot allow al-Qaeda to have a "foothold" in Iraq. Wait a minute, they were not there until this President fell completely into Osama Bin Laden's trap. Every would be terrorist in the world then joined in the fight against America and our soldiers after we invaded Iraq. Now here we are, after 7 years(Bush started planning the war at the time he took office), we are still losing our brave men and women on a daily basis. But this President and the Republicans want to continue fighting Iraq's civil and religious wars. They are willing to kill, for a "legacy." Is that a Pro Life act? Where in the new Bush Bible will we find that? They changed the goal, again.

Give the Iraqi government more time to establish rule. For the third, or was it the fourth goal change, we were supposed to be there for as long as it took to train the Iraqi military. Four(4) years and they cannot get it right? We train our young men and women for six or eight months and send them into battle or they go to train the Iraqi's, who do not get it after 4 years? Who is kidding who?

And the Republicans say it will be a flag of surrender if we leave now. Will it be any different in a year, 2 years, 10 years? How many more American families will we have ruined, or aren't they important? This President and his Republican cohorts, have said we will be surrendering if we leave now. It will not be surrender, except in the minds of people who love war and do not care about the misery we are continuing to create. Every person that has one iota of intelligence, knows we cannot win a military victory, it is a repeat of Korea and even worst, Vietnam. Someone has to have the common sense to STOP THE WAR TODAY.

If we do not stop the war, we should write letters of induction into the service, drafted, for those who think this war is just and the right thing for America. "But some of those people are too old" you say, "they cannot go into the service to fight a war." If they can drive a Hummer on the streets of America, they can get blown up on the streets of Iraq, mothers and grandmothers included, it is time to think of our soldiers, throw out the WAR MONGERS. Grandmothers can take over the mess hall functions, each civilian not hired to cook and clean, will save our country around $400,000.00 per year, in contractor costs. And if you are over 60 years old, remember the new 60 is the old 40, you have to get your son or grandson to take your place. There are no deferments, hardships, college exemptions, the usual hiding places for the well to do. What? Your grandson will not go?

He does not have a choice, he has been drafted! He prefers jail, he may get HURT in Iraq?

Put him there with his grandfather. If all of that is not a good idea, we should start a new draft, for 30 to 60 year olds, but without the usual loopholes for the wealthy and connected. Put people in Iraq who will be quick to question the wisdom of our folly.

"AH HA," you say "We should not be fighting someone else's religious and civil war!"

REALITY will set in, along with the fear that everyone may go to war.

BRING OUR TROOPS HOME TODAY.

FREE TRADE

Then we go back to another calamity this administration has actively pursued, unfettered free trade, and our open border policy with Communist China, India and Indonesia. What? We do not have an open border policy with these people! We are not even their neighbors! Actually, you are right, its better than an open border, there is no border at all, they come and go at will.

- NO IMPORT QUOTAS,
- NO IMPORT CONTROLS,
- NO SAFETY CHECKS,
- NO CHECKS OF ANY KIND,
- QUALITY CONTROL, what's that?

Ever been to a real Chinese factory, the ones that supply the joint venture companies with manufacturing material? You really do not want to go there without prior notice. They do little to ensure their products will be minimally acceptable, never mind have quality. They are emerging from a society that has survived a life of simple means.

Can we expect a peasant from the countryside, that has little exposure to most modern products, to understand what the west considers quality products? Of course not, but don't tell that to our capitalist friends taking up shop there. It will take some time for them to know what modern society produces, but more important, what it expects to receive. Some examples of not understanding or appreciating the impact of materials that are being put into products they build;

Quality Control Supervisor(QA): The paint is not bright enough.

Production Manager(PM): We will put some more lead in it.

QA: The pet food does not meet the weigh standard?
PM: Put some of that scrap ground plastic in it, they are just animals..

QA: The plastic beads on that child's toy will become deadly if swallowed!
PM: Don't tell anyone, it is the hottest toy on the market!

QA: Our defective medicines are causing people to die!
PM: Well we have too many people on the planet anyway!

Actions and thoughts that must be happening in China, I heard one of those very same statements, from Chinese workers during idle conservations. America, home of the best manufacturing facilities and trained factory workers in the world, sold down the drain by greed, to a country still learning the basics of living in a civilized society, that is without a conscious, COMMUNIST CHINA. What are the capitalists in the world thinking, when they are all rushing to Communist China to cash in on slave labor?

Do they think Communists have changed and they no longer seek world domination?

Or the future is for someone else to worry about, we will make a profit at any cost.

Are they all like George Bush, full speed ahead, at any cost or human suffering, my decision is final, even if it is wrong. Poor George. Poor America. Will we trade places once they, China, have all our dollars and America goes into bankruptcy? China, the economic giant, America, fighting communism and essentially fighting for its life? Not a pretty sight.

Should putting all of those real, gross injustices and potential deathtraps in my letters be called pessimistic or realistic? Watching workers pay go down, then stating that American capitalists have betrayed democracy, is that being irresponsible? It should be called a warning to all our people,

WAKE UP AMERICANS BEFORE IT IS TOO LATE.

Politicians have to stop the mindless trade policies that they continue to pursue. They have destroyed our middle class and they do not get it. They have never had to work a day in their lives, so they do not know what a hard days work really is. It is the end of the road for most of what was living wage manufacturing jobs. When will we create new living wage jobs so America can thrive again? It does not look like anytime soon, there is a rough road ahead for America, especially its workers. If the Republicans have anything to say about worker wages, they will never recover.

Maybe we should do to the politicians what the Chinese Communists did during their catastrophic cultural revolution. A program of having the farmers come into the factories, businesses and colleges, and the professors and managers go into the fields so they could taste the hardship while cleansing their brains of western ideas. It produced a famine of untold proportions, 50 to 60 million Chinese starved to death. We would have the same disastrous results.

Just another note on our immigration problems. It has now progressed to the point that illegal aliens are "demanding that they be given rights". Since when does anyone who is an illegal, have rights? In America, when you commit a crime, you lose your rights.

So here we have a double whammy, enter illegally committing a crime, then demand rights. What nonsense! They are criminals, treat them like we do all people from other countries who commit crimes in America, deport them. If we have a prison riot, do we change the laws to suit the rioting prisoners? I don't think so! Are we going to change the laws for these millions of law breakers? I think so!

My take on anyone who is here illegally, has broken the law by doing so, and demanding anything. The only thing I would give them is a bus ride back to where they came from. Every time they have a rally on the streets of America, there should be buses, hundreds if necessary, at the end of that street to take them back to the border they crossed illegally, no questions asked. And that would be a gift.

Everyone says that it is not feasible to deport 10 million people. Airlines move millions of people, every day, around the country and around the world. You mean we could not throw in the extra, a few red eyes a day by all our carriers, that would be required to move a 100,000 a month back to their countries. A million per year, after a couple of years they may get the message that breaking the law is serious, when they are incarcerated, then deported. But we know moving the people back to their country is not the problem at all, its corrupt government, ours and theirs, supporting corrupt corporations, supporting illegal anything, as long as they can make contaminated profits.

LAWYERS

You may have wondered why I did not call out lawyers as part of our problem in America. Well, it is a known fact that practically all politicians are lawyers, therefore

Lawyers are the problem! Do we need to look further? Along the way, another goal should be to elect ordinary citizens, not lawyers, to public office. Don't hold your breath, that will take forever. To be a politician you have to devote time, to the non-paying job of campaigning, for weeks, months or years, to get a job that does not pay very well, compared to successful hi-priced lawyers. Does that make sense? Is it because they are not successful in their law practice? Is it they have too much spare time? My law firm is not doing well, so I will become a politician? Or maybe politics is their free ride to millions of dollars, like most big time politicians, that become very rich on a supposedly modest income. Similar to playing the lottery, only they know theirs is the winning number, P O L I T I C S. Does something smell bad where you are? Without ever even doing a lick of work, lawyers feed at the public trough, they many never leave it for their entire lives. We know what interests the lawyers, it is power, it is influence, it is corruption, call it what you want, big money and greed are behind all politics. A true patriot is hard to find.   Did you ever see a carpenter, plumber, or any "ordinary" person, elected to an office at the national politics level? No? Is it because they are not smart enough, do not work hard enough, or they are not patriotic enough? No, it's the system.

They are not allowed in. They cannot raise millions of dollars for their campaigns, they may never even get off the starting block. Keep the riff-raff out of important government positions, they may not corrupt so quickly, or oh no, they may bring some common sense to government.

There are a host of other problems that our out of control government is not addressing, but my time is short and my energy limited. Many books have been written about them, but they do not seem to illicit any significant response from our leaders.

I said it several times, it cannot be said loud enough, we have been asleep at the wheel, and we have crashed! And if the crash does not wake you up, you must have your IPods turned up to the max or you have already become numb by listening to "music" that has destroyed your ear drums and your mind.

So this is an attempt to show that-me-and my generation have made very wrong decisions, by allowing political "leaders" to force our country onto a path to destruction. We cannot keep going in the same direction. Working people, like our family, need to take charge in America. Since I nor anyone else, can go back and change many decisions we made, maybe by looking at things differently, everyone can make better decisions tomorrow. It is time where everyone who believes in true Democracy, can band together to sweep the corruption out of Washington. It is also time to change our foreign affairs process, we should elect our participants to world politics, not have politicians appoint them. The International Community is where our and the planet's future will be shaped. It is much too important for political chicanery and the appointment of "career diplomats", who usually have one thing in mind, keep my job. Using the present process, they have failed wretchedly, who at this juncture, appear to be diplomatic dunces.

Firmly entrenched, gray haired politicians of today need to become "advisors" to a new generation of younger leaders, who understand how the entire world may be at risk, if someone, somewhere, does not emerge to put all people on track with some common sense.

Well we are off to the start of another week, it is now 2008. Political rhetoric is gaining speed. More big money, by the millions, is pouring into the political campaigns. It will probable be the first time a billion dollars is spent on a presidential election. Politicians have been campaigning non-stop, for months and years. They do that to be appointed to a job that pays 5% of what they are making, or could make, in private life. Quite amazing.

This is America, it once was a great Democratic/capitalistic society. We have allowed GREED and FEAR to destroy our future. And it must be stopped, by everyone who calls themselves Americans! Has anyone, in the past 30 years, been able to rein in healthcare costs using government oversight? Do we have a comprehensive energy program? Do we have anything that is comprehensive, like considering the human aspects of going to war; soldiers families, their jobs, their medical care, their changed lives after they return, and millions of innocent civilians displaced from their country. Shouldn't the plan include withdrawal, never even mentioned for Iraq? Have they or will politicians address

1. Crime,
2. Gangs,
3. Prisons,
4. Drugs.

Is there any indication that a national plan is being developed to correct the downward direction of our country? Everywhere you look, our lives have been pushed to where we have lost control, shoved by our Republican President and the Republicans in Congress. The answer is, we do not have a national plan, for anything.

There is a basic flaw in the notion used by the Republicans when they say they "are strong on terrorism". We went to war and destroyed a country because we had to get even, Bush Sr. was threatened by Saddam. His son, our President, was going to show him who was the boss. The Iraqi people or their leaders had nothing to do with the 3000 people killed in New York by the terrorists, but lets say they did. We destroyed a country of 30,000,000 innocent people for killing 3000 people in this country, and we killed another 3000 Americans (soldiers) while destroying it. What a horrible, horrific, horrendous mistake. Stupidity beyond belief.

Our "trading partners", Mexico, Columbia, etc. want free access to our markets and this Republican administration is making a mad dash to make it happen. These same countries destroy 6 million lives in America, with their "drug trade". Is there something wrong with this picture? Again, for 3000 Americans killed in New York, we annihilate 100,000's of thousands of innocent people in Iraq.

For 6 million citizens destroyed by drugs in America, we provide the countries supplying these drugs, with aid and a welcome as a trading partner. It is a Republican Presidents strategy of hopelessness. The quality of everyone's lifestyle is being altered by illegal drugs, not just those dealing and taking. With 3 million Americans in prison, many for drug related crimes, they are gutting our youth, destroying us from within. If we used the Bush/Chaney doctrine, we should be bombing the countries supplying the drugs that destroys the lives of millions of our young people, unlike Iraq, purported to "kill only 3000". But as always, bombing is never a solution, and never will be the solution to world problems. It should be the option of last resort, for Iraq it certainly was not, they were not even involved. It was the arrogance of a President with little understanding of world affairs, the consequences of going to war or of someone without compassion for ordinary people.

If we didn't consume them, illegal drugs would not be here, so the ultimate culprit is ourselves. Talk to our grandchildren, then everyone has to look at themselves in the mirror, and ask the question, is it me?

Every election has a different, same old, same old, total rhetoric approach. Redefined, reshaped, and reconditioned, but they say nothing about how to address our real, imminent problems. It seems our only true patriots, are on the battlefield in Iraq, fighting for America, while the Republicans/capitalists are fighting against America.

It sounds the opposite of what the Republicans claim, that they support the military. Maybe they support the military/industrial complex, but not those who are losing everything, sometimes their lives, fighting for our country. A reminder, beware of politicians who promise everything, and give you the exact opposite.

President Bush proudly proclaimed "if anyone in my administration is guilty of criminal activity, they will be held responsible!" I guess "held responsible" does not have any tangible meaning, like most political rhetoric. Scooter Libby was convicted of a grievous crime, perjury, to cover for the President and Vice President, while he carried out their illegal commands. Scooter Libby was sentenced to jail for their crimes. He was immediately pardoned by the President, before he set foot in a prison. Responsible? Say what? Is that being "held responsible"? Not even a day in jail, more lies from this Republican administration. When you throw in DeLay, Cummings, Foley, and the whole collection of disgraced corrupt politicians, we have a long line of our leaders, including Bush, who are anything but responsible. Most likely, many dastardly deeds will go down as being orchestrated by the President himself when all the facts are revealed.

We are in serious trouble, mainly because our leaders have no understanding of decency, it seems that being an honorable man is no longer necessary or desirable. All ethical standards are removed when they put their hand on the Bible for the official swearing in ceremonies. It happens every time, so it must be necessary. Lie, Cheat, Deceive and Destroy, are those requisites in the oath necessary to become a politician?

AMERICA, THE LAND OF FEAR.

FEAR. Fear of loosing jobs, based on Republican ideas that if it is not good for industry, it's not good for America. Government oversight is what every Republican calls being anti-jobs and this administration has abandoned any inkling of oversight, yet with

Republican leaders all American manufacturing workers are losing their jobs. Is that another Republican oxymoron, Less government oversight produces jobs. If it is not an oxymoron, it has proven to be up side down Republican political rhetoric "you can count on", while you watch your job disappear.

FEAR. Of workers not being able to provide for their families. As they see their wages and benefits go down, while the cost of everything they need to survive goes up, and not a small amount. The Republican motto "everyone should stand on their own two feet", is for everyone else, not themselves. We should stand on our own two feet while they try to chop our legs off.

FEAR. Of loosing our freedom. George Bush was elected to his second presidential term because we were afraid someone else may not be so brave as George Bush, who promised to destroy all the terrorists and make our country safer. What a mistake for America, his Presidency has put us more at risk than we have ever been.

FEAR. What has been accomplished by this President to ensure our continued freedom and liberty? Anything? Every aspect of a true FREE COUNTRY has been jeopardized by his incompetent leadership and everyone in his administration, right on down to the Federal Prosecutor level. It is the height of political corruption and collusion never seen before, enough for every American to be ashamed of.

The list of things that must be started, changed, improved, or stopped, is long and the road ahead will be difficult for most. This next election will determine if American's workers standard of living will go up or continue to go down, as important as any election in my lifetime. Republicans repeatedly say everything is going good, in spite of the facts showing it to be exactly the opposite, an indication of who is benefiting from the war and our failed economy, and it is not the workers of America.

My checklist for America's future.

- Return RESPECT for your neighbor, your fellow worker, your religion, other religions and everyone in our society.
- Return RESPECT for all people regardless of race, nationality, or ethnic background.

- Return RESPECT for the elderly, the poor and those unable to care for themselves, provide universal healthcare that is long overdue.
- Return RESPECT for our government, enact voter enforced term limits, it may reduce corruption.
- Return RESPECT for our doctors and lawyers, reform our medical system and medical liability laws, but do not let them do it.
- Return RESPECT for our workers, form a national union for all workers, every trade or occupation will have national recognition. We are fighting the biggest union in the world, Communist China, we cannot compete without being organized, with a plan.
- Return RESPECT for our environment, enact an energy program that will put us on the road to renewable and sustainable energy.
- Return RESPECT for AMERICA, at home and abroad, start the American Party, that will represent us in the new world economy, with the good of every American in mind, not just corporations.
- become the UNITED STATES OF AMERICA again, not divided by state, region, north or south.

All things are possible in America, we have proven it time and again. With the internet, and national organizations to make" Return RESPECT" a reality, we can produce amazing results. Its time for individual action, make it happen.

To my Children;

It has been several months since I began writing these letters. Many of the issues I raised have become the dominant headlines, of the presidential campaigns and for the economy. My description of the economy should have been darker, much darker, we are in for significant hardship. The Democrats would be smart to give the next election, by default, to the Republicans, they deserve the mess they created. This Bush Republican administration has botched our country so badly, it may take decades to recover. Again, you will hear the Republicans, blaming the Democrats, for being "fiscally irresponsible", or "soft on terrorism". When they repeat it often enough, some people actually believe them. With the abyss this Republican administration has created, they should be "eating crow" for a long time.

But they won't, they go on like nothing unusual is happening and during the next political speech they will again accuse the Democrats of fiscal irresponsibility, or not getting anything done in Congress, while they filibuster every bill to prevent its passage, legislation that would help the working person. In fact they are saying it today, they are pathetic politicians.

A reminder: If the American people are smart, they would abolish the idea of having the minority rule the majority, Republican control has spelled doom for our society, especially our workers. Put them where they belong, the trash heap of bad social experiments, and come together as one party, the AMERICAN Party, for all our people.

Stay healthy, be kind and love our children,

Love,
Dad/Grandpa
XXXXXXXXXX X2

OUR CHILDREN'S DILEMMA

My children are adults now, and most of my grandchildren are on their own, they ARE the young people who should be asking questions like, who helps the American workers, what political party works for equal opportunity for all, why is healthcare not for everyone and why has our government become so corrupt. All young people face very tough times, me and my generation let our politicians and corporations destroy their future.

An economic tsunami is inundating our working class. Corporations, who are no longer REALLY American, have stolen our lifeboats and gave them to Communist China. Wall Street is now a casino, where the rich play with your retirement and your future, the dealers "make" a billion dollars a year, your money. Politicians spew rhetoric of venom to blind us, so we will not see their duplicitous actions. A war, started by a reckless Republican President is bringing our country down. Fear, greed, crime and disrespect have changed our society.

Letters to my children is my view of a great society betrayed by politicians, capitalists, religious leaders and OURSELVES. We must be The United States of America, not divided as we are, to survive in the new world economy.

- Capitalism, one foot in Communism, the other in Democracy.

- Our President, selling America to fight Iraq's civil and religious wars.
- Healthcare; no money, no treatment. NO Hippocratic Oath here.
- Do you know your NEW Communist and Arab landlords?
- Wages going down instead of up, a Republican victory.
- All young people must prevent the foreboding "GOODBYE MISS AMERICAN DREAM".

www.ingramcontent.com/pod-product-compliance
Lightning Source LLC
Chambersburg PA
CBHW030320290526
45785CB00001B/448